TYPE 2 DIABETES
Cookbook

365 Days of Simple & Fast Diabetic Friendly Recipes (With Colorful Images) for the Newly Diagnosed Warriors!

BONUS: 30-Day Meal Plan to Help Lower Your Blood Sugar Level

Angelina Krystle

Table of Contents

Introduction

Although type 2 diabetes has many consequences, it does not have to be difficult to live with or manage via nutrition. People who suffer from this illness need help every day as they confront their life-long battle against diabetes. This cookbook can provide people struggling with managing their diabetes some guidance and motivation as they work toward living healthier lives, one recipe at a time.

This cookbook is designed for people with diabetes, as well as their families and caregivers. Readers will learn how to avoid the most common pitfalls, such as simple recipes that can be made in large quantities at once. They will also find tips for eating healthy on a budget, tips for food safety and basic diabetes cooking tips.

It is critical that diabetics do not rely on this book to substitute competent medical advice and supervision. This cookbook's objective is to provide readers with practical, easy-to-understand information that they can utilize in their daily lives to safely navigate the world of diabetes. No medical advice should ever be applied without seeking professional guidance first.

This cookbook is designed to be a good read and an easy reference. It also contains pictures for most of the recipes to help readers follow along. The author was diagnosed with type 2 diabetes at the age of 24 and has been on an uphill battle for five years since then. She has one child and is currently single but has previously been married, had kids and enjoyed all those things that life has to offer. She hopes that people with diabetes can embrace the fact that they are not alone in this journey, even though it can be long and difficult.

Whether you are just starting to face the diagnosis of diabetes and are feeling lost, or whether you have had to live with this illness for many years, the Type 2 Diabetes Cookbook will help you to understand what healthy living really means.

Use this cookbook once you have already figured out a few recipes that work for you, or even better, if you are new to the lifestyle. You'll be able to discover what works for you and then connect with others who share your interests. This book was written with the goal of helping people with diabetes lead a healthy lifestyle.

What Is Diabetes Type 2?

High blood glucose level results in type 2 diabetes. Under this condition, the body becomes insulin resistant, which is the body becoming ineffective in using insulin hormone and/or it becomes unable to produce insulin. Insulin hormone is needed for cells to take in glucose (simple sugar) from the blood and then convert it into energy. When the body is unable to digest simple carbohydrates or glucose, type 2 diabetes develops, resulting in high blood glucose levels that can damage bodily organs over time. From this, food for individuals suffering from this type of diabetes becomes a sort of poison. But these people can stay well by lowering their blood sugar by avoiding foods that are high in sugar and by using some medications.

Difference Between Diabetes Type 1 And 2

Although most people are aware that there are two forms of diabetes, not everyone is aware of the differences. Type 1 diabetes, commonly known as insulin-dependent diabetes, is an autoimmune condition that often begins in childhood. It is a condition in which the immune system is attacking and destroying the insulin-producing cells in your pancreas, or the pancreas cells are not functioning effectively, leading to a reduction in the production of insulin. Without insulin, the glucose from carbohydrate foods cannot enter the cells. As a result, blood glucose levels rise, depriving your body's cells and tissues of energy.

Type 2, also known as adult-onset diabetes, is the most common form of diabetes. Type 2 diabetes is largely diet-related and can be caused by different factors. One factor that may cause this type of diabetes is when the pancreas begins to make less insulin. The second possible cause could be that the body becomes resistant to insulin. This means the pancreas is producing insulin, but the body doesn't use it efficiently. Blood sugar levels can get excessively high in both type 1 and type 2 diabetes because the body does not create enough insulin or does not utilize it appropriately. Diabetes can be managed, and diabetic patients can still live a relatively "normal" life.

What Causes Type 2 Diabetes

The number of cases of Type 2 diabetes is soaring related to the obesity epidemic. Type 2 diabetes occurs over time and involves problems getting enough sugar (glucose) into the body's cells. Overweight or obese is the greatest risk factor for Type 2 diabetes. However, the risk is higher if the concentration of weight is around the abdomen as opposed to the thighs and hips. The belly fat that surrounds the liver and abdominal organs is closely linked to insulin resistance. Calories obtained from everyday sugary drinks such as energy drinks, soda, coffee drinks, and processed foods like muffins, doughnuts, cereal, and candy could greatly increase the weight around your abdomen. In addition to eating healthy, cutting back on sugary foods can mean a slimmer waistline as well as a lower risk of diabetes.

Symptoms of Diabetes Type 1 and 2

> Coma
> Itching
> Hunger
> Confusion
> Chest pain
> Headaches
> Blurry vision
> Extreme thirst
> Increased urination
> Fatigue or weakness
> Problems with gums
> Unexplained weight loss
> Problems having an erection
> Nausea, diarrhea, or constipation
> Numbness in the hands and feet

Diabetes is a troublesome disease to live with, regardless of how experienced you are. Adults diagnosed with Type 2 diabetes may have difficulties deciding what to eat and what not to eat. Indeed, even those who have lived with diabetes for quite some time could always use extra guidance and good dieting advice.

Treatment For Diabetes Type 2

Irrespective of type 1 diabetes, type 2 diabetes can be prevented if detected and treated at an early stage. The common treatment for type 2 diabetes includes consuming a low carb, high fiber, and low glycemic index diet along with appropriate and regular physical activities. Some medicines may also be prescribed to diabetic patients, like metformin, which is the most common drug for type 2 diabetes patients and helps the body to respond better to insulin.

How To Prevent and Control Diabetes

How Can Diabetes Be Prevented and Controlled?

Although medical diabetes has no cure, minor lifestyle changes will go a long way in preventing or controlling the disease. While type 1 diabetes requires regular monitoring by a doctor, type 2 diabetes can be controlled by following a healthy lifestyle.

The idea behind this effort is to identify the factors leading to the pre-diabetes phase, which is just before the onset of diabetes. While a person cannot change the genes leading to diabetes, all of us can put the disease in check when it starts to build up excessive blood sugar levels.

Some common things to do to avoid being affected by diabetes:

› Control sugar and carbohydrate intake:

One of the basic steps that your doctor will advise you to take is to limit your intake of sugar, carbs, and processed food items. Elevating your sugar intake will lead to extra pressure on the pancreas to produce insulin from which to derive energy for cells by breaking down the sugars in food. This is one of the common ways to trigger type 2 diabetes in young adults.

› Exercise regularly:

With everything being handed to us on a platter, thanks to the bane of the technologically enabled lifestyle, most of us underutilize our bodies. Lack of physical movement, along with excessive intake of food, has made obesity a household ailment. When a person regularly exercises, the process activates the cells in the body to function even in a condition of low insulin. This allows the insulin to break down the sugar into energy for the cells easily—and, in turn, for the body. A person diagnosed with type 2 diabetes can keep the ailment at bay without taking medication, provided they exercise regularly.

› Drink water:

Water is one of the main elements of the human body and a great caretaker for people diagnosed with diabetes. Drinking water more frequently rather than relying on other beverages helps you avoid the non-essential carbs and sugar that one can intake by drinking aerated drinks. People who consume soda or aerated drinks as their first choice of beverage are more likely to develop LADA, a type 1 diabetes.

› Lose weight:

Being overweight is one of the precursors to type 2 diabetes. Therefore, a person should be careful to ensure that they are not becoming obese. One of the easiest methods is to check your body mass index regularly. The reading will give you a fair idea of whether you are starting to grow extra fat in your body. Even a small amount of fat gain greatly affects your chances of attracting diabetes. Follow a healthy diet plan and start working out as soon as possible.

› Do not smoke:

Other than causing life-threatening cancer, smoking wildly affects a diabetic patients. Not just smoking but also second-hand smoke has been shown to have signs of aggravating type 2 diabetes. Get counseling, if necessary, but quit smoking. Need we say more?

Preventing Pre-diabetes

Prevention is always better than cure. If you can stop yourself from developing diabetes before you actually have it, you will be saving yourself from a lifetime of being a prisoner to your body. It isn't even all that difficult.

Research has proven that if you are pre-diabetic, you can decrease the chances of the onset of type 2 diabetes by losing 7% of your body mass and following a moderate exercise routine. Something as easy as a daily walk around your neighborhood could save your life.

Should you already have type 2 diabetes, this is not a death sentence. You are not a "Deadman walking," and by maintaining a healthy weight, engaging in regular exercise, and eating wisely, you can improve your body's acceptance of insulin, thereby decreasing the sugar levels in your blood. You can lock the moody diabetes teenager away and live a healthy and fulfilling life.

Diabetes Treatment Options

Diabetes treatment isn't about getting rid of a problem in your life. Instead, it is about management. Once diagnosed as diabetic, most people don't get magically diabetic. This means you can't hide in your closet and refuse to deal with the reality and impact of diabetes on your health.

You need to use medical treatment, dietary treatment, and a combination of physical activity and balanced mental health to keep yourself in good health.

Medical Treatment

When treating and managing your diabetes, you need to know your blood sugar levels. If you don't know your "sweet spot," you won't be able to regulate your intake of carbohydrates or sucrose and the production of insulin. For type 1 diabetes, this becomes crucial as you may need to take insulin injections to help regulate your blood sugar.

Testing your blood sugar levels isn't like randomly checking your bank balance at the ATM. You need to be organized—your life may depend on it.

When you are diagnosed as a person with diabetes, you need to be prepared and diligent in your testing:

> Always keep your testing equipment with you.
> Use new testing strips and keep them away from heat and sunlight.
> Make testing part of your life and test at the same times each day.
> Schedule maintenance and calibration of your testing machine regularly.
> Keep track of your results in a notebook or app on your phone.
> Manage your testing site effectively and safely.

Knowing your sugar levels helps you plan your diet and enables you to manage your diabetes with careful nutrition planning.

Dietary Treatment

Medical Nutrition Therapy (MNT) is when your healthcare practitioner advises you about which foods to avoid, which to bulk on, and the times and quantities of your meals. This helps your body work in sync with your unique diabetes diagnosis. No two diabetics are identical, and while you can maybe sneak a candy bar once in a while, your neighbor may have fits if they have even one sniff of chocolate.

In numerous tests and research studies, the DASH diet, the Mediterranean diet, and vegetarian or plant-based foods have been found to be the most beneficial to those managing their diabetes. After all, you are what you eat.

A structured meal plan can really help you get those blood sugar numbers under control. By following a specially crafted MNT, you can cut down on the blood glucose levels in your body, reducing your blood sugar levels, and maintaining optimal health. This puts you in control of your diabetes with every spoonful you eat.

Physical Activity and Mental Health

Get up and move. Not only will this help you produce endorphins that will help you feel better, but it will also reduce your blood glucose levels. Even if you don't necessarily lose weight with your physical activities, it is still a win for anyone living with diabetes.

Try to get at least two and a half hours of physical activity throughout the week. Be careful to spread that feel-good movement over a couple of days. Never do more than two consecutive days of exercise. Not only will this help prevent injuries, but it will also help you form healthy physical activity habits.

Living with diabetes can be overwhelming, and you need to cultivate a strong mental approach. Type 2 diabetes is particularly rough on your emotions, and you may suffer from mood swings and feel stressed. Engage in self-care, and you will be able to remain mentally and emotionally fit and on top of your game.

If you are going to let sugar become your boss, then your health will suffer. Diabetes management is important to preserve your health and well-being. Stay positive and live responsibly. There's no reason to feel stressed or depressed (though you may feel like this at times). When in doubt, reach out. There are amazing online support groups. And in many urban centers, there are also diabetes clinics where you can get access to resources and helpful advice from medical professionals.

Diabetes is absolutely treatable, and by following a controlled diet, working with your healthcare practitioners, and maintaining a healthy weight and exercise program (and, if necessary, taking medication), you can beat diabetes.

What To Eat and What to Avoid

What to Eat:

> Healthy nuts fats such as almonds, olive oil, walnuts, cashews and peanuts.

> Fresh fruits, vegetables, and whole fruit.

> High-fiber cereals and slices of bread are made from whole grains.

> Fish and shellfish.

> Organic chicken or turkey.

> Protein from eggs, low-fat dairy, beans, and unsweetened yogurt.

What to Avoid:

> Processed or fast food, especially those high in sugar.

> Sugary cereals, white bread, refined pasta, or rice.

> Red or processed meat.

> Low-fat products with added sugar, such as fat-free yogurt.

The real meat in this book is its use of simple sentences to explain diabetes-related topics such as understanding type 2 diabetes, designing a menu, how much food should be eaten in a day, food to eat and avoid, and a healthy meal plan for Type 2 diabetes patient.

Carbohydrate counting is going to be part of your life now. The recipes in this book are made up of generous amounts of fruits, vegetables, and fiber, which are likely to reduce the risk of cardiovascular diseases and certain types of cancer. The recipes in these books are similar to what you will find in The American Diabetes Association Diabetes Comfort Food Cookbook by Robin Webb, M.S. Embracing a healthy eating plan is a best and fastest way to keep your blood glucose level under control and prevent diabetes complications. Type 2 Diabetics Cookbook for Beginners is here to help you navigate your way around diabetes management by providing a 30-day meal plan made from 150 delicious and healthy recipes to help you develop good eating habits and ultimately manage your diabetes.

Breakfast

– RECIPES –

Apple Topped French Toast

Preparation time: 10 minutes

Cooking time: 40 minutes

Servings: 2

Ingredients:

> 1 apple, peel and slice thin
> 1 egg
> ¼ cup skim milk
> 2 tbsp. margarine, divided

What you'll need from the store cupboard:

> 4 slices of Healthy Loaf Bread
> 1 tbsp. Splenda brown sugar
> 1 tsp vanilla
> ¼ tsp cinnamon

Directions:

1. Melt 1 tablespoon margarine in a large skillet over med-high heat. Add apples, Splenda, and cinnamon and cook, frequently stirring, until apples are tender.
2. In a shallow dish, whisk together egg, milk, and vanilla.
3. Melt the remaining margarine in a separate skillet over med-high heat. Dip each slice of bread in the egg mixture and cook until golden brown on both sides.
4. Place two slices of French toast on plates, and top with apples. Serve immediately.

Nutrition:

Calories: 394 Fat: 23 g Protein: 10 g Carbs: 27 g
Fiber: 5 g Sugar: 19 g Sodium: 265 mg

Breakfast Sandwich

Preparation time: 10 minutes

Cooking time: 30 minutes

Servings: 2

Ingredients:

> 2 oz/60g cheddar cheese
> 1/6 oz/30g smoked ham
> 2 tbsp butter
> 4 eggs

Directions:

1. Fry all the eggs and sprinkle the pepper and salt on them.
2. Place an egg down as the sandwich base. Top with the ham and cheese and a drop or two of Tabasco.
3. Place the other egg on top and enjoy.

Nutrition:

Calories: 600 Fat: 50 g Protein: 12 g Carbs: 7 g
Fiber: 0 g Sugars: 1.38 g Sodium: 308 mg

Buckwheat Porridge

Preparation time: 10 minutes

Cooking time: 30 minutes

Servings: 2

Ingredients:

> 1½ cups water
> 1 cup buckwheat groats, rinsed
> ¾ teaspoon vanilla extract
> ½ teaspoon ground cinnamon
> ¼ teaspoon salt
> 2 tablespoons maple syrup
> 1 ripe banana, peeled and mashed
> 1½ cups unsweetened soy milk
> 1 tablespoon peanut butter
> 1/3 cup fresh strawberries, hulled and chopped

Directions:

1. Place the water, buckwheat, vanilla extract, cinnamon, and salt in a pan and bring to a boil.
2. Now, adjust the heat to medium-low and simmer for about 6 minutes, stirring occasionally.
3. Stir in maple syrup, banana, and soy milk, and simmer, covered for about 6 minutes.
4. Remove the pan of porridge from heat and stir in peanut butter.
5. Serve warm with the topping of strawberry pieces.

Nutrition:

Calories: 453 Fat: 9.4 g Protein: 16.2 g Carbs: 82.8 g
Fiber: 9.4 g Sugar: 28.8 g Sodium: 374 mg

Cinnamon Apple Oatmeal

Preparation time: 5 minutes

Cooking time: 5 minutes

Servings: 2

Ingredients:

> ¼ cup apple juice
> 1 cup of water
> 1 apple, cored and chopped
> 1 teaspoon ground cinnamon
> 1 cup milk
> 2/3 cups of rolled oats

Directions:

1. Add the apple juice, water, and apples into a pot. Bring your apple mixture to a boil over high heat and then stir in your rolled oats and cinnamon.
2. Return your apple mixture to a boil, then reduce to low heat, and simmer until oats are thick for about 5 minutes.
3. Spoon into serving bowls, and pour the milk over the servings.

Nutrition:

Calories: 217 Fat: 38.1 g Protein: 7.8 g Carbs: 1 g
Fiber: 2.4 g Sugar: 19 g Sodium: 131 mg

Egg Salad Sandwiches

Preparation time: 10 minutes

Cooking time: 0 minutes

Servings: 2

Ingredients:

> 8 large hardboiled eggs
> 3 tablespoons plain low-fat Greek yogurt
> 1 tablespoon mustard
> ½ teaspoon freshly ground black pepper
> 1 teaspoon chopped fresh chives
> 4 slices 100% whole-wheat bread
> 2 cups fresh spinach, loosely packed

Direction:

1. Peel the eggs and cut them in half.
2. In a large bowl, mash the eggs with a fork, leaving chunks.
3. Add the yogurt, mustard, pepper, and chives, and mix.
4. For each portion, layer 1 slice of bread with one-quarter of the egg salad and spinach.

Nutrition: Calories: 278 Fat: 12.1 g Protein: 20.1 g Carbs: 23.1 g Fiber: 2.9 g Sugar: 3.1 g Sodium: 365 mg

Egg White Zucchini Frittata

Preparation time: 10 minutes

Cooking time: 5 minutes

Servings: 2

Ingredients:

> 4 egg whites
> 1 zucchini, shaved into thin strips
> ½ clove garlic, minced
> 1 tablespoon shallots, minced
> 1 teaspoon olive oil
> ½ teaspoon thyme, fresh chopped
> sea salt and black pepper as needed

Directions:

1. Heat your olive oil into a nonstick skillet over medium-high heat. Add to the skillet the shallot and garlic, cooking for about 5 minutes or until soft.
2. Whisk the egg whites, thyme, salt and pepper in a small bowl. Mix into your zucchini mixture.
3. Cook your frittata over low heat for about 2 minutes, then flip over and cook for an additional minute. Serve and enjoy!

Nutrition: Calories: 137 Fat: 5 g Protein: 16.5 g Carbs: 7.9 g Fiber: 1.4 g Sugar: 21g Sodium: 89 mg

Fish With Fresh Herb Sauce

Preparation time: 10 minutes

Cooking time: 10 minutes

Servings: 2

Ingredients:

> 2 (4-oz) cod fillets, rinsed and patted dry
> 1/3 cup fresh cilantro
> 1/4 tsp cumin (ground)
> 1 tbsp red onion
> 2 tsp extra virgin olive oil
> 1 tsp red wine vinegar
> 1 small clove of garlic
> 1/8 tsp salt
> 1/8 black pepper

Directions

1. Combine chopped cilantro, finely chopped onion, oil, red wine vinegar, minced garlic, and salt.
2. Sprinkle both sides of fish fillets with cumin and pepper.
3. Cook fillets 4 minutes per side. Top each fillet with cilantro mixture.

Nutrition: Calories: 90 Fat: 4 g Protein: 6 g Carbs: 3 g Fiber: 2.4 g Sugar: 21.4 g Sodium: 241 mg

Hawaiian Breakfast Bake

Preparation time: 10 minutes

Cooking time: 40 minutes

Servings: 2

Ingredients:

> 6 slice ham, sliced thin
> 6 eggs
> ¼ cup reduced-fat cheddar cheese, grated

What you'll need from the store cupboard:

> 6 pineapple slices
> 2 tbsp. salsa
> ½ tsp seasoning blend, salt-free

Directions:

1. Heat oven to 350 degrees.
2. Line 6 muffin cups or ramekins with sliced ham. Layer with cheese, salsa, and pineapple.
3. Crack one egg into each cup, and sprinkle with seasoning blend.
4. If using ramekins, place them on a baking sheet, bake 20-25 minutes or until egg whites are completely set but yolks are still soft. Serve immediately.

Nutrition: Calories: 135 Fat: 8 g Protein: 12 g Carbs: 5 g Fiber: 1 g Sugar: 3 g Sodium: 681 mg

Jicama Hash Browns

Preparation time: 10 minutes

Cooking time: 40 minutes

Servings: 2

Ingredients:

> 2 cups jicama, peeled and grated
> ½ small onion, diced

What you'll need from the store cupboard

> 1 tbsp. vegetable oil
> A pinch of salt to taste
> A pinch of pepper to taste

Directions:

1. Add the oil to a large skillet and heat over med-high heat.
2. Add the onion and cook until translucent.
3. Add the jicama and salt and pepper to taste. Cook until nicely browned on both sides. Serve immediately.

Nutrition: Calories: 113 Fat: 7g Protein: 1g Carbs: 6 g Fiber: 6 g Sugar: 3g Sodium: 7 mg

Mushroom and Spinach Scrambled Eggs

Preparation time: 10 minutes

Cooking time: 8 minutes

Servings: 2

Ingredients:

> 2 large egg whites
> 2 large eggs
> 1 teaspoon of butter
> ½ cup mushrooms, thinly sliced and fresh
> ½ cup baby spinach, fresh chopped
> 2 tablespoons provolone cheese, shredded
> sea salt and black pepper as needed

Directions:

1. In a bowl, add your egg whites, eggs, salt, and pepper, then blend.
2. In a nonstick skillet, heat the butter over medium-high heat. Add your mushrooms and cook for about 5 minutes or until tender.
3. Add the spinach to the skillet and stir until wilted. Reduce heat to medium-low
4. Add your egg mixture to the skillet and stir in the eggs until no liquid remains. Stir in the cheese.
5. Add your scrambled eggs to a serving dish and enjoy!

Nutrition: Calories: 162 Fat: 42.5 g Protein: 13 g Carbs: 2 g Fiber: 4 g Sugar: 24 g Sodium: 231 mg

Oatmeal Yogurt Breakfast

Preparation time: 20 minutes

Cooking time: 0 minutes

Servings: 2

Ingredients:

> 1 cup milk
> 1 cup quick-cooking oats
> ½ cup Greek yogurt
> 1 banana, mashed
> 2 tablespoons low-fat peanut butter
> 3 tablespoons flaxseed meal

Directions:

1. Whisk your oats, banana, yogurt, flaxseed meal, peanut butter, and milk in a mixing bowl. Place your mixture in the fridge for about 15 minutes. Serve and enjoy!

Nutrition: Calories: 242 Fat: 11.4 g Protein: 9.5 g Carbs: 27.4 g Fiber: 3.4 g Sugar: 26 g Sodium: 325 mg

Pumpkin Spice French Toast

Preparation time: 10 minutes

Cooking time: 40 minutes

Servings: 2

Ingredients:

> 6 eggs
> 1 ½ cup skim milk

What you'll need from the store cupboard:

> 8 slices of Healthy Loaf Bread
> ¼ cup pumpkin
> 1 tsp salt
> 1 tsp pumpkin pie spice
> 1 tsp vanilla
> Butter flavored cooking spray

Directions:

1. In a large bowl, whisk together all ingredients, except bread, until combined. Add the bread slices and toss to coat.
2. Spray a large, nonstick skillet with cooking spray and place over medium heat. Add bread, two slices, or what fits in the pan, at a time and cook 2-3 minutes per side. Serve as is or with sugar-free maple syrup.

Nutrition: Calories: 295 Fat: 20 g Protein: 17 g Carbs: 10 g Fiber 2: g Sugar: 5 g Sodium: 989 mg

Pumpkin Walnut Oatmeal

Preparation time: 5 minutes

Cooking time: 5 minutes

Servings: 2

Ingredients:

> 1 cup of soy milk
> ½ cup old-fashioned rolled oats
> ¼ cup canned pumpkin puree
> 1 tablespoon walnuts, chopped
> 3 dashes of ground cinnamon
> ½ teaspoon honey

Directions:

1. Mix the soy milk, oats, pumpkin puree, and cinnamon in a pan.
2. Bring your mixture to a gentle boil, then reduce heat to low and simmer for 5 minutes.
3. Add mixture to a serving bowl and garnish with walnuts and honey. Serve and enjoy!

Nutrition: Calories: 244 Fat: 10 g Protein: 10.9 g Carbs: 31 g Fiber: 1.4 g Sugar: 22 g Sodium: 193 mg

Raisin French Toast

Preparation time: 10 minutes

Cooking time: 4 minutes

Servings: 2

Ingredients:

> 4 slices of cinnamon-raisin bread
> ½ cup liquid egg substitute
> ½ cup fat-free milk
> 2 teaspoons Splenda
> ½ teaspoon vanilla extract

Directions:

1. Coat a nonstick skillet with cooking spray.
2. In a mixing bowl, beat your egg substitute, vanilla, milk, and Splenda until smooth. Pour into a shallow dish.
3. Coat both sides of your bread with egg mixture. Over medium heat, cook for about 4 minutes per side or until browned. Serve and enjoy!

Nutrition: Calories: 107 Fat: 1.5 g Protein: 6 g Carbs: 17 g Fiber: 5 g Sugar: 15 g Sodium: 281 mg

Salad With Ranch

Preparation time: 10 minutes

Cooking time: 0 minutes

Servings: 2

Ingredients:

- 1/2 (10-oz) pkg iceberg lettuce
- 1/2 cup cucumber
- 1/4 cup grape tomatoes
- 2 tbsp refrigerated yogurt (sugar-free)
- 1/4 tsp pepper

Directions

1. Combine chopped lettuce, chopped cucumber, and halved tomatoes in a bowl.
2. Drizzle with dressing, and sprinkle with pepper.
3. Toss.
4. You can lose weight and have diabetes! This dish is perfect for weight loss.

Nutrition: Calories: 80 Fat: 2 g Protein: 12 g

Carbs: 0.1 g Fiber: 1.4 g Sugar: 32. g Sodium: 134 mg

Salty Macadamia Chocolate Smoothie

Preparation time: 10 minutes

Cooking time: 0 minutes

Servings: 2

Ingredients:

- 2 tablespoons macadamia nuts
- 1/3 cup chocolate whey protein powder, low carb
- 1 cup almond milk, unsweetened

Directions:

1. Add the listed ingredients to your blender and blend until you have a smooth mixture
2. Chill and enjoy it!

Nutrition: Calories: 165 Fat: 2 g Protein: 12 g

Carbs: 1 g Fiber: 1 g Sugars: 21 g Sodium: 170 mg

Savory Keto Pancake

Preparation time: 10 minutes

Cooking time: 30 minutes

Servings: 2

Ingredients:

> ¼ cup almond flour
> 1 ½ tbsp unsalted butter
> 2 eggs
> 2 oz cream cheese, softened

Directions:

1. Bring out a bowl, crack eggs in it, whisk well until fluffy, and then whisk in flour and cream cheese until well combined.
2. Bring out a skillet pan, put it over medium heat, add butter and when it melts, drop pancake batter into four sections, spread it evenly, and cook for 2 minutes per side until brown.

Nutrition: Calories: 166.8 Fat: 15 g Protein: 5.8 g Cabs: 1.8 g Fiber: 0.8 g Sugars: 1.65 g Sodium: 230 mg

Steel-Cut Oatmeal Bowl with Fruit and Nuts

Preparation time: 10 minutes

Cooking time: 30 minutes

Servings: 2

Ingredients:

> 1 cup steel-cut oats
> 2 cups almond milk
> ¾ cup water
> 1 teaspoon ground cinnamon
> ¼ teaspoon salt
> 2 cups chopped fresh fruit, such as blueberries, strawberries, raspberries, or peaches
> 1/2 cup chopped walnuts
> ¼ cup chia seeds

Directions:

1. In a medium saucepan over medium-high heat, combine the oats, almond milk, water, cinnamon, and salt. Bring to a boil, reduce the heat to low, and simmer for 15 to 20 minutes until the oats are softened and thickened.
2. Top each bowl with 1/2 cup of fresh fruit, 2 tablespoons of walnuts, and 1 tablespoon of chia seeds before serving.

Nutrition: Calories: 288 Fat: 11 g Protein: 10 g Carbs: 38 g Fiber: 10 g Sugar: 7 g Sodium: 329 mg

Strawberry Kiwi Smoothies

Preparation time: 10 minutes

Cooking time: 40 minutes

Servings: 2

Ingredients:

> 2 kiwi, peel & quarter
> 6 oz. strawberry yogurt
> 1 cup strawberries, frozen
> ½ cup skim milk

What you'll need from the store cupboard:

> 2 tbsp. honey

Directions:

1. Place all ingredients in a blender and process until smooth.
2. Pour into glasses and serve immediately.

Nutrition: Calories: 120 Fat: 1 g Protein: 3 g

Carbs: 26 g Fiber: 2 g Sugar: 23 g Sodium: 28 mg

Sweet Potato Waffles

Preparation time: 10 minutes

Cooking time: 30 minutes

Servings: 2

Ingredients:

> 1 medium sweet potato, peeled, grated, and squeezed
> 1 teaspoon fresh thyme, minced
> 1 teaspoon fresh rosemary, minced
> 1/8 teaspoon red pepper flakes, crushed
> Salt and ground black pepper, as required

Directions:

1. Preheat the waffle iron and then grease it.
2. In a large bowl, add all ingredients and mix till well combined.
3. Place half of the sweet potato mixture into preheated waffle iron and cook for about 8-10 minutes or until golden brown.
4. Repeat with the remaining mixture. Serve warm.

Nutrition: Calories: 72 Fat: 0.3 g Protein: 1.6 g

Carbs: 16.3 g Fiber: 3 g Sugar: 4.9 g Sodium: 28 mg

Vegetables And Salads

– RECIPES –

Baked Potato Topped with Cream cheese 'n Olives

Preparation time: 15 minutes

Cooking time: 40 minutes

Servings: 2

Ingredients:

- ¼ teaspoon onion powder
- 1 medium russet potato, scrubbed and peeled
- 1 tablespoon chives, chopped
- 1 tablespoon Kalamata olives
- 1 teaspoon olive oil
- 1/8 teaspoon salt
- a dollop of vegan butter
- a dollop of vegan cream cheese

Directions:

1. Place inside the air fryer basket and cook for 40 minutes. Be sure to turn the potatoes once halfway.
2. Place the potatoes in a mixing bowl and pour in olive oil, onion powder, salt, and vegan butter.
3. Preheat the air fryer to 4000F.
4. Serve the potatoes with vegan cream cheese, Kalamata olives, chives, and other vegan toppings that you want.

Nutrition: Calories: 504 Fat: 21.53 g

Protein: 9.31 g Carbs: 68.34 g Fiber: 5.2 g

Sugars: 2.38 g Sodium: 391 mg

Bell Pepper Black Olive Salad

Preparation time: 10 minutes

Cooking time: 0 minutes

Servings: 2

Ingredients:

- 2 cups chopped iceberg lettuce
- 10 cherry tomatoes, halved
- 1 cup pitted black olives, chopped
- 6 ounces ham, chopped
- ½ red onion, chopped
- 1 red bell pepper, seeded and chopped
- 10 basil leaves, torn
- ¼ cup Italian Vinaigrette

Directions:

1. 1. In a large bowl, combine the lettuce, tomatoes, olives, ham, onion, bell pepper, and basil leaves.
2. 2. Toss with the vinaigrette just before serving.

Nutrition: Calories: 434 Fat: 31 g Protein: 22 g

Carbs: 17 g Fiber: 5 g Sugar: 5.61 g Sodium: 228 mg

Bell Pepper-Corn Wrapped in Tortilla

Preparation time: 5 minutes

Cooking time: 15 minutes

Servings: 2

Ingredients:

> 1 small red bell pepper, chopped
> 1 small yellow onion, diced
> 1 tablespoon water
> 2 cobs grilled corn kernels
> 4 large tortillas
> 4 pieces of commercial vegan nuggets, chopped
> mixed greens for garnish

Directions:

1. Preheat the air fryer to 4000F.
2. In a skillet heated over medium heat, water sautés the vegan nuggets together with the onions, bell peppers, and corn kernels. Set aside.
3. Place filling inside the corn tortillas.
4. Fold the tortillas and place them inside the air fryer and cook for 15 minutes until the tortilla wraps are crispy. Serve with mixed greens on top.

Nutrition: Calories: 548 Fat: 20.76 g

Protein: 46.73 g Carbs: 43.54 g Fiber: 3.1 g

Sugars: 2.14 g Sodium: 424 mg

Black Bean Burger with Garlic-Chipotle

Preparation time: 10 minutes

Cooking time: 20 minutes

Servings: 2

Ingredients:

> ½ cup corn kernels
> ½ teaspoon chipotle powder
> ½ teaspoon garlic powder
> ¾ cup salsa
> 1 ¼ teaspoon chili powder
> 1 ½ cup rolled oats
> 1 can of black beans, rinsed and drained
> 1 tablespoon soy sauce

Directions:

1. In a mixing bowl, combine all ingredients and mix using your hands.
2. Form small patties using your hands and set them aside.
3. Brush patties with oil if desired.
4. Place the grill pan in the air fryer and place the patties on the grill pan accessory. Close the lid and cook for 20 minutes on each side at 330°F.

Nutrition: Calories: 395 Fat: 5.8 g

Protein: 24.3 g Carbs: 52.2 g Fiber: 3.6 g

Sugars: 1.88 g Sodium: 234 mg

Brussels Sprouts with Balsamic Oil

Preparation time: 5 minutes

Cooking time: 15 minutes

Servings: 2

Ingredients:

> ¼ teaspoon salt
> 1 tablespoon balsamic vinegar
> 2 cups Brussels sprouts, halved
> 2 tablespoons olive oil

Directions:

1. Preheat the air fryer for 5 minutes.
2. Mix all ingredients in a bowl until the zucchini fries are well coated.
3. Place in the air fryer basket.
4. Close and cook for 15 minutes at 3500F.

Nutrition: Calories: 82 Fat: 6.8 g

Protein: 1.5 g Carbs: 4.6 g Fiber: 1.7 g Sugars: 1.57 g

Sodium: 185 mg

Cheesy Mushroom and Pesto Flatbreads

Preparation time: 10 minutes

Cooking time: 13 to 17 minutes

Servings: 2

Ingredients:

> 1 teaspoon extra-virgin olive oil
> ½ red onion, sliced
> ½ cup sliced mushrooms
> Salt and freshly ground black pepper to taste
> ¼ cup store-bought pesto sauce
> 2 whole-wheat flatbreads
> ¼ cup shredded Mozzarella cheese

Directions:

1. Preheat the oven to 350°F (180°C).
2. Heat the olive oil in a small skillet over medium heat. Add the onion slices and mushrooms to the skillet, and sauté for 3 to 5 minutes, stirring occasionally, or until they start to soften. Season with salt and pepper.
3. Meanwhile, spoon 2 tablespoons of pesto sauce onto each flatbread and spread it all over. Evenly divide the mushroom mixture between two flatbreads, then scatter each top with 2 tablespoons of shredded cheese.
4. Transfer the flatbreads to a baking sheet and bake until the cheese melts and bubbles, about 10 to 12 minutes.
5. Let the flatbreads cool for 5 minutes and serve warm.

Nutrition: Calories: 346 Fat: 22.8 g Protein: 14.2 g

Carbs: 27.6 g Fiber: 7.3 g Sugar: 4.0 g Sodium: 790 mg

Chestnut Lettuce Wraps

Preparation time: 10 minutes

Cooking time: 0 minutes

Servings: 2

Ingredients:

> 1 tablespoon freshly squeezed lemon juice
> 1 teaspoon curry powder
> 1 teaspoon reduced-sodium soy sauce
> ½ teaspoon sriracha (or to taste)
> ½ cup canned water chestnuts, drained and chopped
> 2 (2.6-ounce/73.7 g) packages of tuna packed in water, drained
> 2 large butter lettuce leaves

Directions:

1. In a medium bowl, whisk together lemon juice, curry powder, soy sauce, and sriracha.
2. Add the water chestnuts and tuna. Stir to combine.
3. Serve wrapped in the lettuce leaves.

Nutrition: Calories: 271 Fat: 14 g Protein: 19 g
Carbs: 18 g Fiber: 3 g Sugar: 8.1 g Sodium: 627 mg

Chicken, Cantaloupe, Kale and Almond Salad

Preparation time: 10 minutes

Cooking time: 0 minutes

Servings: 2

Ingredients:

Salad:

> 4 cups chopped kale, packed
> 1½ cups diced cantaloupe
> 1½ cups shredded rotisserie chicken
> ½ cup sliced almonds
> ¼ cup crumbled feta

Dressing:

> 2 teaspoons honey
> 2 tablespoons extra-virgin olive oil
> 2 teaspoons apple cider vinegar or freshly squeezed lemon juice

Direction:

Make the Salad:

1. Divide the kale into three portions. Layer 1/3 of the cantaloupe, chicken, almonds, and feta on each portion.
2. Drizzle some of the dressing over each portion of the salad. Serve immediately.
3. Make the Dressing
4. In a small bowl, whisk together the honey, olive oil, and vinegar.

Nutrition: Calories: 396 Fat:22 g Protein: 27 g
Carbs: 24g Fiber: 4 g Sugars: 12 g Sodium: 236 mg

Creamy Cauliflower and Broccoli

Preparation time: 4 minutes

Cooking time: 16 minutes

Servings: 2

Ingredients:

- 1-pound cauliflower florets
- 1-pound broccoli florets
- 2 ½ tablespoons sesame oil
- 1/2 teaspoon smoked cayenne pepper
- 3/4 teaspoon sea salt flakes
- 1 tablespoon lemon zest, grated
- 1/2 cup Colby cheese, shredded

Directions:

1. Prepare the cauliflower and broccoli using your favorite steaming method. Then, drain them well; add the sesame oil, cayenne pepper, and salt flakes.
2. Air-fry at 390 degrees F for approximately 16 minutes; make sure to check the vegetables halfway through the cooking time.
3. Afterward, stir in the lemon zest and Colby cheese; toss to coat well and serve immediately!

Nutrition: Calories: 133 Fat: 9.0 g Carbs: 9.5 g Protein: 5.9 g Fiber: 3.6 g Sugars: 3.2 g Sodium: 405 mg

Cucumber-Carrot Salad

Preparation time: 30 minutes

Cooking time: 10 minutes

Servings: 2

Ingredients:

- 1/4 cup seasoned rice vinegar
- 1 teaspoon white sugar
- 1/2 teaspoon vegetable oil
- 1/4 teaspoon grated peeled ginger
- 1/4 teaspoon salt
- 1 cup sliced carrot
- 2 tablespoons sliced green onions
- 2 tablespoons minced red bell pepper
- 1/2 cucumber - halved lengthwise, seeded, and sliced

Directions:

1. Whisk rice vinegar, sugar, vegetable oil, ginger, and salt together in a bowl until sugar and salt are dissolved into a smooth dressing.
2. Toss the carrot, green onion, bell pepper, and cucumber in the dressing to coat evenly.
3. Cover bowl with plastic wrap and refrigerate until chilled, about 30 minutes.

Nutrition: Calories: 40 Fat: 1.57 g Protein: 1.03 g Carbs: 5.3 g Fiber: 0.9 g Sugar: 19 g Sodium: 297 mg

Cucumber Tomato Avocado Salad

Preparation time: 10 minutes

Cooking time: 0 minutes

Servings: 2

Ingredients:

- 1 cup cherry tomatoes, halved
- 1 large cucumber, chopped
- 1 small red onion, thinly sliced
- 1 avocado, diced
- 2 tablespoons chopped fresh dill
- 2 tablespoons extra-virgin olive oil
- Juice of 1 lemon
- ¼ teaspoon salt
- ¼ teaspoon freshly ground black pepper

Direction:

1. In a large mixing bowl, combine the tomatoes, cucumber, onion, avocado, and dill.
2. In a small bowl, combine the oil, lemon juice, salt, and pepper, and mix well.
3. Drizzle the dressing over the vegetables and toss to combine. Serve.

Nutrition: Calories: 151 Fat: 12 g Protein: 2 g
Carbs: 11 g Fiber: 4 g Sugars: 4 g Sodium: 128 mg

Egg Pea Mix wrapped in Kale Leaves

Preparation time: 10 minutes

Cooking time: 0 minutes

Servings: 2

Ingredients:

- 1 teaspoon Dijon mustard
- 1 tablespoon chopped fresh dill
- ½ teaspoon sea salt
- ¼ teaspoon paprika
- 4 large hard-boiled eggs, chopped
- 1 cup shelled fresh peas
- 2 tablespoons finely chopped red onion
- 2 large kale leaves

Directions:

1. In a medium bowl, whisk together mustard, dill, salt, and paprika.
2. Stir in the eggs, peas, and onion.
3. Serve wrapped in kale leaves.

Nutrition: Calories: 295 Fat: 18 g Protein: 17 g
Carbs: 18 g Fiber: 4 g Sugar: 3.7 g Sodium: 620 mg

Fruity Tuna Salad

Preparation time: 1 hour

Cooking time: 0 minutes

Servings: 2

Ingredients:

> 1 (5-ounce) can tuna, drained
> 1/2 cup chopped dates
> 3/4 cup chopped celery
> 1/2 large apple - peeled, cored, and diced
> 1/4 cup lemon yogurt
> 1 1/2 teaspoons minced onions
> 1 teaspoon lemon juice
> 1/2 teaspoon ground curry powder

Directions:

1. In a sizable bowl, mix the tuna, dates, celery, and apple.
2. In another bowl, whisk together the yogurt, onion, lemon juice, and curry powder. Pour over tuna mixture and gently toss to coat. Refrigerate for one hour or until chilled.

Nutrition: Calories: 194 Fat: 0.91 g

Protein: 12.94 g Carbs: 37.06 g Fiber: 4.9 g

Sugar: 22.4 g Sodium: 170 mg

Grilled Portobello and Zucchini Burger

Preparation time: 5 minutes

Cooking time: 10 minutes

Servings: 2

Ingredients:

> 2 large portabella mushroom caps
> ½ small zucchini, sliced
> 2 slices of low-fat cheese
> Spinach

What you'll need from the store cupboard:

> 2 100% whole wheat sandwich thins
> 2 tsp roasted red bell peppers
> 2 tsp olive oil

Directions:

1. Heat grill, or charcoal, to med-high heat.
2. Lightly brush mushroom caps with olive oil. Grill mushroom caps and zucchini slices until tender, about 3-4 minutes per side.
3. Place on sandwich thin. Top with sliced cheese, roasted red bell pepper, and spinach. Serve.

Nutrition: Calories: 177 Fat: 3 g Protein: 15 g

Carbs: 26 g Fiber: 8 g Sugar: 3 g Sodium:67 mg

Honey Roasted Carrots

Preparation time: 15 minutes

Cooking time: 12 minutes

Servings: 2

Ingredients:

> 454g of rainbow carrots, peeled and washed
> 15 ml of olive oil
> 30 ml honey
> 2 sprigs of fresh thyme
> Salt and pepper to taste

Directions:

1. Wash the carrots and dry them with a paper towel. Leave aside.
2. Preheat the air fryer for a few minutes at 180#.
3. Place the carrots in a bowl with olive oil, honey, thyme, salt, and pepper. Place the carrots in the air fryer at 1800C for 12 minutes. Be sure to shake the baskets in the middle of cooking.

Nutrition: Calories: 123 Fat: 42g Carbohydrate: 9g Protein: 1g Fiber: 2.1g Sugar: 24 g Sodium: 313 mg

Kale and Carrot Veggie Soup

Preparation time: 10 minutes

Cooking time: 15 minutes

Servings: 2

Ingredients:

> 2 tablespoons extra-virgin olive oil
> 1 onion, finely chopped
> 1 carrot, chopped
> 1 cup chopped kale (stems removed)
> 3 garlic cloves, minced
> 1 cup canned lentils, drained and rinsed
> 1 cup unsalted vegetable broth
> 2 teaspoons dried rosemary (or 1 tablespoon chopped fresh rosemary)
> ½ teaspoon sea salt
> ¼ teaspoon freshly ground black pepper

Directions:

1. In a large pot over medium-high heat, heat the olive oil until it shimmers.
2. Add the onion and carrot and cook, stirring, until the vegetables begin to soften, about 3 minutes.
3. Add the kale and cook for 3 minutes more. Add the garlic and cook, constantly stirring, for 30 seconds.
4. Stir in the lentils, vegetable broth, rosemary, salt, and pepper. Bring to a simmer. Simmer, occasionally stirring, for 5 minutes more.

Nutrition: Calories: 160 Fat: 7 g Protein: 6 g Carbs: 19 g Fiber: 6 g Sugar: 15 g Sodium: 187 mg

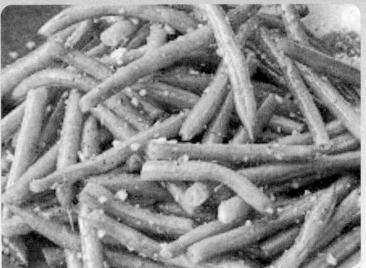

Lemon-Basil Strawberry Salad

Preparation time: 20 minutes

Cooking time: 0 minutes

Servings: 2

Ingredients:

> 1-pound fresh strawberries, sliced
> 1 tablespoon white sugar
> teaspoon 1/8 salt
> 2 tablespoons fresh basil leaves, chiffonade
> 2 teaspoons balsamic vinegar
> 1 teaspoon lemon juice

Direction:

1. Combine strawberries, sugar, and salt in a bowl. Set aside for 10 minutes.
2. Combine basil, balsamic, and lemon juice in another bowl. Pour over strawberries and toss to coat. Serve.

Nutrition: Calories: 41 Fat: 0.49 g Protein: 0.81 g Carbs: 9.35 g Fiber: 2.3 g Sugar: 14 g Sodium: 79 mg

Simple Green Beans with Butter

Preparation time: 2 minutes

Cooking time: 10 minutes

Servings: 2

Ingredients:

> 3/4-pound green beans, cleaned
> 1 tablespoon balsamic vinegar
> 1/4 teaspoon kosher salt
> 1/2 teaspoon mixed peppercorns, freshly cracked
> 1 tablespoon butter
> 2 tablespoons toasted sesame seeds to serve

Directions:

1. Set your Air Fryer to cook at 390 degrees F.
2. Mix the green beans with all of the above ingredients, apart from the sesame seeds. Set the timer for 10 minutes.
3. Meanwhile, toast the sesame seeds in a small-sized nonstick skillet; make sure to stir continuously.
4. Serve sautéed green beans on a nice serving platter sprinkled with toasted sesame seeds. Bon appétit!

Nutrition: Calories: 73 Fat: 3.0 g Protein: 1.6 g Carbs: 6.1 g Fiber: 2.1 g Sugars: 1.2 g Sodium: 194 mg

Sofrito Steak Salad

Preparation time: 10 minutes
Cooking time: 15 minutes
Servings: 2
Ingredients:

> 4 ounces (113 g) recaíto cooking base
> 2 (4-ounce / 113-g) flank steaks
> 8 cups fresh spinach, loosely packed
> ½ cup sliced red onion
> 2 cups diced tomato
> 2 avocados, diced
> 2 cups diced cucumber
> 1/3 cup crumbled feta

Direction:

1. Heat a large skillet over medium-low heat. When hot, pour in the recaíto cooking base, add the steaks, and cover. Cook for 8 to 12 minutes.
2. Meanwhile, divide the spinach into four portions. Top each portion with one-quarter of the onion, tomato, avocados, and cucumber.
3. Remove the steak from the skillet, and let it rest for about 2 minutes before slicing. Place one-quarter of the steak and feta on top of each portion.

Nutrition: Calories: 344 Fat: 18 g Protein: 25 g Carbs: 18 g Fiber: 8 g Sugars: 6 g Sodium: 382 mg

Tart Cabbage Side Salad

Preparation time: 10 minutes
Cooking time: 0 minutes
Servings: 2
Ingredients:

> 2 cups coleslaw mix
> 1 tomato, diced small
> 1/2 cucumber, diced small
> 1 tablespoon rice vinegar
> 1 teaspoon Dijon mustard
> 1/2 teaspoon agave nectar
> 1 pinch salt and ground black pepper to taste

Direction:

1. Toss coleslaw mix, tomato, and cucumber together in a mixing bowl.
2. Whisk vinegar, Dijon mustard, and agave nectar together in a bowl until emulsified; season with salt and pepper. Drizzle dressing over the vegetable mixture. Turn the salad with a fork until vegetables are evenly coated in dressing.

Nutrition: Calories: 97 Fat: 0.31 g Protein: 1.28 g Carbs: 23.42 g Fiber: 1.3 g Sugar: 24 g Sodium: 84 mg

Tomato, Peach and Strawberry Salad

Preparation time: 15 minutes

Cooking time: 0 minutes

Servings: 2

Ingredients:

- 4 cups mixed spring greens
- 4 large ripe plum tomatoes, thinly sliced
- 4 large ripe peaches, pitted and thinly sliced
- 12 ripe strawberries, thinly sliced
- ½ Vidalia onion, thinly sliced
- 2 tablespoons white balsamic vinegar
- 2 tablespoons extra-virgin olive oil
- Freshly ground black pepper, to taste

Direction:

1. Put the greens in a large salad bowl, and layer the tomatoes, peaches, strawberries, and onion on top.
2. Dress with vinegar and oil, toss together, and season with pepper.

Nutrition: Calories: 127 Fat: 5 g Protein: 4 g Carbs: 19 g Fiber: 5 g Sugars: 13 g Sodium: 30 mg

Young Kale and Cabbage Salad

Preparation time: 15 minutes

Cooking time: 0 minutes

Servings: 2

Ingredients:

- 2 bunches of baby kale, thinly sliced
- ½ head green savoy cabbage, cored and thinly sliced
- ¼ cup apple cider vinegar
- Juice of 1 lemon
- 1 teaspoon ground cumin
- ¼ teaspoon smoked paprika
- 1 medium red bell pepper, thinly sliced
- 1 cup toasted peanuts
- 1 garlic clove, thinly sliced

Direction:

1. In a large salad bowl, toss the kale and cabbage together.
2. In a small bowl, to make the dressing, whisk the vinegar, lemon juice, cumin, and paprika together.
3. Pour the dressing over the greens and gently massage with your hands.
4. Add the pepper, peanuts, and garlic, and toss to combine.

Nutrition: Calories: 199 Fat: 12 g Protein: 10 g Carbs: 17 g Fiber: 5 g Sugars: 4 g Sodium: 46 mg

Beef, Pork and Lamb

– RECIPES –

Beef and Zucchini Meatballs

Preparation time: 5 minutes

Cooking Time: 25 minutes

Servings: 2

Ingredients:

> Ground beef 1 pound (454 g)
> Grated zucchini 1 cup
> Salt ¼ tsp
> Pepper ¼ tsp

Directions:

1. Preheat the oven to 400 F (204 °C).
2. In a bowl, mix all **Ingredients:** and shape them into 20 meatballs.
3. Place on a baking sheet and bake for 23-25 minutes.
4. Serve hot.

Nutrition: Calories: 397 Fat: 24 g Protein: 36 g Carbs: 4 g Fiber: 1.6 g Sugar: 16 g Sodium: 145 mg

Beef Burrito Bowl

Preparation time: 5 minutes

Cooking time: 15 minutes

Servings: 2

Ingredients:

> 1 pound (454 g) 93% lean ground beef
> 1 cup canned low-sodium black beans, drained and rinsed
> ¼ teaspoon ground cumin
> ¼ teaspoon chili powder
> ¼ teaspoon garlic powder
> ¼ teaspoon onion powder
> ¼ teaspoon salt
> 1 head romaine or preferred lettuce, shredded
> 2 medium tomatoes, chopped
> 1 cup shredded cheddar cheese or packaged cheese blend

Direction:

1. Heat a large skillet over medium-low heat. Put the beef, beans, cumin, chili powder, garlic powder, onion powder, and salt into the skillet, and cook for 8 to 10 minutes, until cooked through. Stir occasionally.
2. Divide the lettuce evenly between four bowls. Add one-quarter of the beef mixture to each bowl and top with one-quarter of the tomatoes and cheese.

Nutrition: Calories: 351 Fat: 18 g Protein: 35 g Carbs: 14 g Fiber: 6 g Sugars: 4 g Sodium: 424 mg

Beef Korma Curry

Preparation time: 10 minutes

Cooking time: 17-20 minutes

Servings: 2

Ingredients:

> 1 pound (454 g) sirloin steak, sliced
> 1/2 cup yogurt
> 1 tablespoon curry powder
> 1 tablespoon olive oil
> 1 onion, chopped
> 2 cloves garlic, minced
> 1 tomato, diced
> 1/2 cup frozen baby peas, thawed

Directions:

1. In a medium bowl, combine the steak, yogurt, and curry powder. Stir and set aside.
2. In a metal bowl, combine the olive oil, onion, and garlic. Bake at 350 °F (177 °C) for 3 to 4 minutes or until crisp and tender.
3. Add the steak along with the yogurt and the diced tomato. Bake for 12 to 13 minutes or until the steak is almost tender.
4. Stir in the peas and bake for 2 to 3 minutes or until hot.

Nutrition: Calories: 299 Fats: 11 g Proteins: 38 g
Carbs: 9 g Fibers: 2 g Sugars: 3 g Sodium: 100 mg

Chipotle Chili Pork Chops

Preparation time: 5 minutes

Cooking time: 20 minutes

Servings: 2

Ingredients:

> Juice and zest of 1 lime
> 1 tablespoon extra-virgin olive oil
> 1 tablespoon chipotle chili powder
> 2 teaspoons minced garlic
> 1 teaspoon ground cinnamon
> Pinch sea salt
> 4 (5-ounce / 142-g) pork chops, about 1 inch thick
> Lime wedges, for garnish

Direction:

1. Combine the lime juice and zest, oil, chipotle chili powder, garlic, cinnamon, and salt in a resealable plastic bag. Add the pork chops. Remove as much air as possible and seal the bag.
2. Marinate the chops in the refrigerator for at least 4 hours and up to 24 hours, turning them several times.
3. Preheat the oven to 400°F (205°C) and set a rack on a baking sheet. Let the chops rest at room temperature for 15 minutes, then arrange them on the rack and discard the remaining marinade.
4. Roast the chops until cooked through, turning once, about 10 minutes per side. Serve with lime wedges.

Nutrition: Calories: 204 Fat: 9 g Protein: 30 g
Carbs: 1 g Fiber: 0 g Sugars: 1 g Sodium: 317 mg

Country-Style Pork Ribs

Preparation time: 5 minutes

Cooking time: 20-25 minutes

Servings: 2

Ingredients:

> 12 country-style pork ribs, trimmed of excess fat
> 2 tablespoons cornstarch
> 2 tablespoons olive oil
> 1 teaspoon dry mustard
> 1/2 teaspoon thyme
> 1/2 teaspoon garlic powder
> 1 teaspoon dried marjoram
> Pinch salt
> Freshly ground black pepper, to taste

Directions:

1. Place the ribs on a clean work surface.
2. In a small bowl, combine the cornstarch, olive oil, mustard, thyme, garlic powder, marjoram, salt, and pepper, and rub into the ribs.
3. Abode the ribs in the air fryer basket and roast at 400 °F (204 °C) for 10 minutes.
4. Carefully turn the ribs using tongs and roast for 10 to 15 minutes or until the ribs are crisp and register an internal temperature of at least 150 °F (66 °C).

Nutrition: Calories: 579 Fat: 44 g Proteins: 40 g Carbs: 4 g Fiber: 0 g Sugars: 0 g Sodium: 155 mg

Couscous and Sweet Potatoes with Pork

Preparation time: 20 minutes

Cooking time: 10 minutes

Servings: 2

Ingredients:

> 1¼ cup uncooked couscous
> 1 pound pork tenderloin, thinly sliced
> 1 medium sweet potato, peeled, cut into julienne strips
> 1 cup chunky-style salsa
> ½ cup water
> 2 tablespoons honey
> ¼ cup chopped fresh cilantro

Direction:

1. Cook couscous as directed on the package.
2. While couscous is cooking, spray a 12-inch skillet with cooking spray. Cook pork in a skillet over medium heat 2 to 3 minutes, occasionally stirring, until brown.
3. Stir sweet potato, salsa, water, and honey into pork. Heat to boiling; reduce heat to medium. Cover and cook for 5 to 6 minutes, occasionally stirring, until potato is tender. Sprinkle with cilantro. Serve pork mixture over couscous.

Nutrition: Calorie: 320 Fat: 4 g Protein: 23 g Carbs: 48 g Fiber: 3 g Sugars: 11 g Sodium: 420 mg

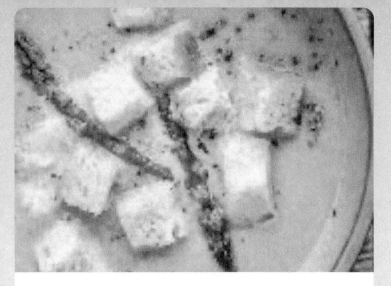

Creamy Asparagus Veggie Soup Bowl

Preparation time: 10 minutes

Cooking time: 20 minutes

Servings: 4

Ingredients:

> 2 pounds (907 g) of fresh asparagus, remove the bottom and cut into small pieces
> 1 yellow onion, diced
> 1 small lemon, zest and juice
> 1 teaspoon fresh thyme, diced fine
> 4 cup low sodium vegetable broth
> 3 tablespoons olive oil
> 3 cloves garlic, diced fine
> Salt and ground black pepper to taste

Direction:

1. Heat oil in a large saucepan over medium-high heat. Add asparagus and onion and cook, occasionally stirring, until nicely browned, about 5 minutes. Add garlic and cook 1 minute more.
2. Stir in remaining and bring to a boil. Reduce heat, and simmer for 12 to 15 minutes or until asparagus is soft.
3. Use an immersion blender and process until smooth. Salt and ground black pepper to taste and serve.

Nutrition: Calories: 170 Fat: 11.0 g Protein: 6.2 g Carbs: 17.1 g Fiber: 6.2 g Sugar: 7.1 g Sodium: 185 mg

Curried Pork and Vegetable Skewers

Preparation time: 15 minutes

Cooking time: 15 minutes

Servings: 2

Ingredients:

> ¼ cup plain nonfat Greek yogurt
> 2 tablespoons curry powder
> 1 teaspoon garlic powder
> 1 teaspoon ground turmeric
> Zest and juice of 1 lime
> ¼ teaspoon salt
> Pinch freshly ground black pepper

> 1 pound (454 g) boneless pork tenderloin, cut into bite-size pieces
> 1 red bell pepper, seeded and cut into 2-inch squares
> 1 green bell pepper, seeded and cut into 2-inch squares
> 1 red onion, quartered and split into segments

Direction:

1. In a large bowl, mix the yogurt, curry powder, garlic powder, turmeric, lime zest, lime juice, salt, and pepper.
2. Add the pieces of pork tenderloin to the bowl, and stir to coat. Refrigerate for at least 1 hour or as long as 6 hours.
3. Preheat a grill or broiler to medium. Thread the pork pieces, bell peppers, and onions onto skewers.
4. Grill or broil for 12 to 15 minutes, flipping every 3 or 4 minutes until the pork is cooked through. Serve.

Nutrition: Calories: 175 Fat: 3 g Protein: 27 g Carbs: 10 g Fiber: 3 g Sugars: 4 g Sodium: 188 mg

Diet Boiled Ribs

Preparation time: 10 minutes

Cooking time: 30 minutes

Servings: 2

Ingredients:

> 400 g pork ribs
> 1 teaspoon black pepper
> 1 g bay leaf
> 1 teaspoon basil
> 1 white onion
> 1 carrot
> 1 teaspoon cumin
> 700 ml of water

Directions:

1. Cut the ribs into the portions and sprinkle them with black pepper.
2. Take a big saucepan and pour water into it.
3. Add the ribs and bay leaf.
4. Peel the onion and carrot and add them to the water with the meat.
5. Sprinkle it with cumin and basil.
6. Cook it on medium heat in the air fryer for 30 minutes.

Nutrition: Calories: 294 Fat: 18 g Protein: 27 g Carbs: 5 g Fiber: 3.6 g Sugar: 19 g Sodium: 362 mg

Fried Pork Chops

Preparation time: 10 minutes

Cooking time: 35 minutes

Servings: 2

Ingredients:

> 3 cloves of ground garlic
> 2 tbsp. olive oil
> 1 tbsp. of marinade
> 4 thawed pork chops

Directions:

1. Mix the cloves of ground garlic, marinade, and oil. Then apply this mixture to the chops.
2. Put the chops in the air fryer at 3600C for 35 minutes

Nutrition: Calories: 118 Fat: 3.41 g Protein: 20.99 g Carbs: 0 g Fiber: 3.1 g Sugar: 0 g Sodium: 342 mg

Lamb Burgers with Mushrooms and Cheese

Preparation time: 15 minutes
Cooking time: 15 minutes
Servings: 2
Ingredients:

> 8 ounces (227 g) grass-fed ground lamb
> 8 ounces (227 g) of brown mushrooms, finely chopped
> ¼ teaspoon salt
> ¼ teaspoon freshly ground black pepper
> ¼ cup crumbled goat cheese
> 1 tablespoon minced fresh basil

Direction:

1. In a large mixing bowl, combine the lamb, mushrooms, salt, and pepper, and mix well.
2. In a small bowl, mix the goat cheese and basil.
3. Form the lamb mixture into 4 patties, reserving about ½ cup of the mixture in the bowl. In each patty, make an indentation in the center and fill with 1 tablespoon of the goat cheese mixture. Use the reserved meat mixture to close the burgers. Press the meat firmly to hold it together.
4. Heat the barbecue or a large skillet over medium-high heat. Add the burgers and cook for 5 to 7 minutes on each side until cooked through. Serve.

Nutrition: Calories: 173 Fat: 13 g Protein: 11 g Carbs: 3 g Fiber: 0 g Sugars: 1 g Sodium: 154 mg

Lamb Kofta Meatballs with Cucumber Salad

Preparation time: 10 minutes
Cooking time: 15 minutes
Servings: 2
Ingredients:

> ¼ cup red wine vinegar
> Pinch red pepper flakes
> 1 teaspoon sea salt, divided
> 2 cucumbers, peeled and chopped
> ½ red onion, finely chopped
> 1 pound (454 g) ground lamb
> 2 teaspoons ground coriander
> 1 teaspoon ground cumin
> 3 garlic cloves, minced
> 1 tablespoon fresh mint, chopped

Direction:

1. Preheat the oven to 375°F (190°C). Line a rimmed baking sheet with parchment paper.
2. In a medium bowl, whisk together the vinegar, red pepper flakes, and ½ teaspoon of salt. Add the cucumbers and onion and toss to combine. Set aside.
3. In a large bowl, mix the lamb, coriander, cumin, garlic, mint, and remaining ½ teaspoon of salt. Form the mixture into 1-inch meatballs and place them on the prepared baking sheet.
4. Bake until the lamb reaches 140°F (60°C) internally, about 15 minutes. Serve with the salad on the side.

Nutrition: Calories: 345 Fat: 27 g Protein: 20 g Carbs: 7 g Fiber: 1 g Sugars: 3 g Sodium: 362 mg

Lemon and Honey Pork Tenderloin

Preparation time: 5 minutes

Cooking time: 10 minutes

Servings: 2

Ingredients:

> 1 (1-pound / 454-g) pork tenderloin, cut into 1/2-inch slices
> 1 tablespoon olive oil
> 1 tablespoon freshly squeezed lemon juice
> 1 tablespoon honey
> 1/2 teaspoon grated lemon zest
> 1/2 teaspoon dried marjoram
> Pinch salt
> Freshly ground black pepper, to taste

Directions:

1. Put the pork tenderloin slices in a medium bowl.
2. In a minor bowl, combine the olive oil, lemon juice, honey, lemon zest, marjoram, salt, and pepper. Mix.
3. Pour this marinade over the tenderloin slices and massage gently with your hand to work it into the pork.
4. Place the pork in the air fryer basket and roast at 400 °F (204 °C) for 10 minutes or until the pork registers at least 145 °F (63 °C) using a meat thermometer.

Nutrition: Calories: 208 Fats: 8 g Proteins: 30 g Carbs: 5 g Fibers: 0 g Sugar: 4 g Sodium: 104 mg

Lemon Greek Beef and Vegetables

Preparation time: 10 minutes

Cooking time: 9-19 minutes

Servings: 2

Ingredients:

> 1/2 pound (227 g) 96% lean ground beef
> 2 medium tomatoes, chopped
> 1 onion, chopped
> 2 garlic cloves, minced
> 2 cups fresh baby spinach
> 2 tablespoons freshly squeezed lemon juice
> 1/3 cup low-sodium beef broth
> 2 tablespoons crumbled low-sodium feta cheese

Directions:

1. In a baking pan, crumble the beef. Place in the air fryer basket. Air fry at 370 °F (188 °C) for 3 to 7 minutes, stirring once during cooking until browned. Drain off any fat or liquid.
2. Swell the tomatoes, onion, and garlic to the pan. Air fry for 4 to 8 minutes more, or until the onion is tender.
3. Add the spinach, lemon juice, and beef broth.
4. Air fry for 2 to 4 minutes more, or until the spinach is wilted. Sprinkle with the feta cheese and serve immediately.

Nutrition: Calories: 98 Fat: 1 g Protein: 15 g Carbs: 5 g Fibers: 1 g Sugars: 2 g Sodium: 123 mg

Low-Fat Steak

Preparation time: 25 minutes

Cooking time: 10 minutes

Servings: 2

Ingredients:

> 400 g beef steak
> 1 teaspoon white pepper
> 1 teaspoon turmeric
> 1 teaspoon cilantro
> 1 teaspoon olive oil
> 3 teaspoon lemon juice
> 1 teaspoon oregano
> 1 teaspoon salt
> 100 g water

Directions:

1. Rub the steaks with white pepper and turmeric and put them in the big bowl.
2. Sprinkle the meat with salt, oregano, cilantro and lemon juice.
3. Leave the steaks for 20 minutes.
4. Combine olive oil and water and pour it into the bowl with the steaks.
5. Grill the steaks in the air fryer for 10 minutes from both sides.
6. Serve it immediately.

Nutrition: Calories: 268 Fats: 10 g Proteins: 41 g
Carbs: 2 g Fiber: 3.7 g Sugar: 15 g Sodium: 532 mg

Meatloaf Reboot

Preparation time: 20 minutes

Cooking time: 9 minutes

Servings: 2

Ingredients:

> 4 slices of leftover meatloaf, cut about 1-inch thick.

Directions:

1. Preheat your air fryer to 350 degrees.
2. Spray each side of the meatloaf slices with cooking spray. Add the slices to the air fryer and cook for about 9 to 10 minutes. Don't turn the slices halfway through the cooking cycle because they may break apart. Instead, keep them on one side to cook to ensure they stay together

Nutrition: Calories: 201 Fat: 5 g Protein: 38 g
Carbs: 9.6 g Fiber: 5.3 g Sugar: 1.8g Sodium: 143 mg

Mustard Glazed Pork Chops

Preparation time: 5 minutes

Cooking time: 25 minutes

Servings: 2

Ingredients:

> ¼ cup Dijon mustard
> 1 tablespoon pure maple syrup
> 2 tablespoons rice vinegar
> 4 bone-in, thin-cut pork chops

Direction:

1. Preheat the oven to 400°F (205°C).
2. In a small saucepan, combine the mustard, maple syrup, and rice vinegar. Stir to mix and bring to a simmer over medium heat. Cook for about 2 minutes until just slightly thickened.
3. In a baking dish, place the pork chops and spoon the sauce over them, flipping to coat.
4. Bake, uncovered, for 18 to 22 minutes until the juices run clear.

Nutrition: Calories: 257 Fat: 7 g Protein: 39 g
Carbs: 7 g Fiber: 0 g Sugars: 4 g Sodium: 466 mg

Parmesan-Crusted Pork Chops

Preparation time: 10 minutes

Cooking time: 25 minutes

Servings: 2

Ingredients:

> Nonstick cooking spray
> 4 bone-in, thin-cut pork chops
> 2 tablespoons butter
> ½ cup grated Parmesan cheese
> 3 garlic cloves, minced
> ¼ teaspoon salt
> ¼ teaspoon dried thyme
> Freshly ground black pepper, to taste

Direction:

1. Preheat the oven to 400°F (205°C). Line a baking sheet with parchment paper and spray with nonstick cooking spray.
2. Arrange the pork chops on the prepared baking sheet, so they do not overlap.
3. In a small bowl, combine the butter, cheese, garlic, salt, thyme, and pepper. Press 2 tablespoons of the cheese mixture onto the top of each pork chop.
4. Bake for 18 to 22 minutes until the pork is cooked through and its juices run clear. Set the broiler to high, then broil for 1 to 2 minutes to brown the tops.

Nutrition: Calories: 332 Fat: 16 g Protein: 44 g
Carbs: 1 g Fiber: 0 g Sugars: 0 g Sodium: 440 mg

Peppered Beef with Greens and Beans

Preparation time: 10 minutes

Cooking time: 20 minutes

Servings: 2

Ingredients:

> 1 (½-pound / 227-g, ½-inch-thick) boneless beef sirloin, halved
> 2 teaspoons coarsely ground black pepper, divided
> ¼ cup tomato sauce
> 2 tablespoons red wine vinegar
> 1 teaspoon dried basil
> 3 cups (1 bunch) chopped kale
> 1 cup chopped green beans
> ¾ cup chopped red bell pepper or yellow bell pepper
> ¼ cup chopped onion

Direction:

1. Rub each side of the steak halves with ½ teaspoon of coarsely ground pepper.
2. Heat a 10-inch nonstick skillet over medium heat. Add the beef. Cook for 8 to 12 minutes, turning once halfway through.
3. Add the tomato sauce, red wine vinegar, and basil. Stir to combine.
4. Add the kale, green beans, bell pepper, and onion. Stir to mix with the sauce. Reduce the heat to medium-low. Cook for about 5 minutes, uncovered, or until the vegetables are tender and the beef is cooked at medium doneness (160°F / 71°C). Serve immediately and enjoy!

Nutrition: Calories: 372 Fat: 17 g Protein: 35 g Carbs: 22 g Fiber: 6 g Sugars: 4 g Sodium: 349 mg

Pork Chops with Raspberry-Chipotle Sauce and Herbed Rice

Preparation time: 25 minutes

Cooking time: 10 minutes

Servings: 2

Pork Chops:

> 4 bone-in pork rib chops, about ¾ inch thick
> ½ teaspoon garlic-pepper blend
> 1 tablespoon canola oil

Raspberry-Chipotle Sauce:

> 1/3 cup all-fruit raspberry spread
> 1 tablespoon water
> 1 tablespoon raspberry-flavored vinegar
> 1 large or 2 small chipotle chiles in adobo sauce, finely chopped (from a 7-ounce can)

Herbed Rice:

> 1 package (8.8 ounces) quick-cooking (ready in 90 seconds) whole-grain brown rice
> ¼ teaspoon salt-free garlic-herb blend
> ½ teaspoon lemon peel
> 1 tablespoon chopped fresh cilantro

Direction:

1. Sprinkle pork with garlic pepper. In 12-inch nonstick skillet, heat oil over medium-high heat. Add pork to oil. Cook 8 to 10 minutes, turning once until pork is no longer pink and the meat thermometer inserted in the center reads 145°F. Remove from skillet to serving platter (reserve pork drippings); keep warm.
2. Meanwhile, in a small bowl, stir raspberry spread, water, vinegar and chile; set aside. Make rice as directed on the package. Stir in remaining rice ingredients; keep warm.
3. In a skillet with pork drippings, pour the raspberry mixture. Cook and stir over low heat for about 1 minute or until sauce is bubbly and slightly thickened. Serve pork chops with sauce and rice.

Nutrition: Calories: 370 Fat: 12 g Protein: 31 g Carbs: 34 g Fiber: 0 g Sugars: 12 g Sodium: 140 mg

Pork Medallions with Cherry Sauce

Preparation time: 25 minutes

Cooking time: 6 to 8 minutes

Servings: 2

Ingredients:

> 1 pork tenderloin (1 to 1¼ lb.), cut into ½-inch slices
> ½ teaspoon garlic-pepper blend
> 2 teaspoons olive oil
> ¾ cup cherry preserves
> 2 tablespoons chopped shallots
> 1 tablespoon Dijon mustard
> 1 tablespoon balsamic vinegar
> 1 clove of garlic, finely chopped

Direction:

1. Sprinkle both sides of pork with the garlic-pepper blend. 2 In a 12-inch skillet, heat 1 teaspoon of the oil over medium-high heat. Add pork; cook 6 to 8 minutes, turning once, until pork is browned and the meat thermometer inserted in the center reads 145°F.

2. Remove pork from skillet; keep warm. 3 In the same skillet, mix the remaining teaspoon of oil, the preserves, shallots, mustard, vinegar and garlic, scraping any brown bits from the bottom of the skillet. Heat to boiling.

3. Reduce heat; simmer uncovered for 10 minutes or until reduced to about ½ cup. Serve sauce over pork slices.

Nutrition: Calorie: 330 Fat: 7 g Protein: 23 g
Carbs: 44 g Fiber: 1 g Sugars: 30 g Sodium: 170 mg

Pork on a Blanket

Preparation time: 10 minutes

Cooking time: 10 minutes

Servings: 2

Ingredients:

> ½ puff pastry sheet, defrosted
> 16 thick smoked sausages
> 15 ml of milk

Directions:

1. Preheat la air fryer to 200°C and set the timer to 5 minutes.

2. Cut the puff pastry into 64 x 38 mm strips.

3. Place a cocktail sausage at the end of the puff pastry and roll around the sausage, sealing the dough with some water.

4. Brush the top (with the seam facing down) of the sausages wrapped in milk and place them in the preheated air fryer. Cook at 200°C for 10 minutes or until golden brown.

Nutrition: Calories: 381 Fat: 5 g Protein: 38 g
Carbs: 9.6 g Fiber: 4.6 g Sugar: 1.8 g Sodium: 424 mg

Quick & Juicy Pork Chops

Preparation time: 10 minutes

Cooking time: 12 minutes

Servings: 2

Ingredients:

> 4 pork chops
> 1 tsp. olive oil
> 1 tsp. onion powder
> 1 tsp. paprika
> Pepper to taste
> Salt to taste

Directions:

1. Cover pork chops with olive oil and season with paprika, onion powder, pepper, and salt.
2. Place the dehydrating tray in a multi-level air fryer basket and place the basket in the instant pot.
3. Place pork chops on dehydrating tray.
4. Seal pot with air fryer lid and select air fry mode, then set the temperature to 380 °F and timer for 12 minutes. Turn pork chops halfway through. Serve and enjoy.

Nutrition: Calories: 270 Fat: 21g Protein: 18g Carbs: 1g Fiber: 3.6 g Sugars: 0.3g Sodium: 325 mg

Roll-Ups from Mexico

Preparation time: 10 minutes

Cooking time: 0 minutes

Servings: 2

Ingredients:

> 1 teaspoon of olive oil
> 2 large heads 2 romaine lettuce leaves, large ribs removed
> 2 (8 inches) whole wheat 96% fat-free heart-healthy tortillas, such as Mission brand
> 8 ounces of extra-lean ground beef (95% lean)
> 1/3 cup of chopped tomato (1 small)
> 1/3 cup of chopped red sweet pepper
> 1 tablespoon of red wine vinegar
> 1 teaspoon of ground cumin

Direction:

1. In a skillet, cook ground beef over medium-high heat until golden brown, using a spoon to break up meat as it cooks.
2. Drain off the fat. Stir the vinegar, tomato, cumin, sweet pepper, and oil into the meat in the skillet.
3. Place a turbot leaf on each tortilla.
4. Spoon half of the cooked ground meat mixture onto each lettuce leaf. Completely roll up each filled tortilla. If desired, secure roll-ups with skewers.

Nutrition: Calories: 296 Fat: 9.8 g Protein: 28.1 g Carbs: 28.3 g Fiber: 7.2 g Sugars: 2 g Sodium: 154 mg

Rosemary Lamb Chops

Preparation time: 30 minutes

Cooking time: 20 minutes

Servings: 2 to 3

Ingredients:

> 2 teaspoons oil
> 1/2 teaspoon ground rosemary
> 1/2 teaspoon lemon juice
> 1 pound (454 g) lamb chops, approximately 1-inch thick
> Salt and pepper to taste
> Cooking spray

Directions:

1. Mix the oil, rosemary, and lemon juice and rub them into all sides of the lamb chops. Season to taste with salt and pepper.
2. For best flavor, cover lamb chops and allow them to rest in the fridge for 15 to 20 minutes.
3. Spray the air fryer basket with nonstick spray and place lamb chops in it.
4. Air fry at 360 °F (182 °C) for approximately 20 minutes. This will cook chops to medium. The meat will be juicy but have no remaining pink. Air fry for 1 to 2 minutes longer for well-done chops. For rare chops, stop cooking after about 12 minutes and check for doneness.

Nutrition: Calories: 237 Fat: 13 g Protein: 30 g Carbs: 0 g Fibers: 0 g Sugars: 0 g Sodium: 116 mg

Za'atar Lamb Chops

Preparation time: 10 minutes

Cooking time: 10 minutes

Servings: 2

Ingredients:

> 4 lamb loin chops
> 1/2 Tbsp Za'atar
> 1 Tbsp fresh lemon juice
> 1 tsp. olive oil
> 2 garlic cloves, minced
> Pepper to taste
> Salt to taste

Directions:

1. Coat lamb chops with oil and lemon juice and rub with Za'atar, garlic, pepper, and salt.
2. Place the dehydrating tray in a multi-level air fryer basket and place the basket in the instant pot.
3. Place lamb chops on dehydrating tray.
4. Seal pot with air fryer lid and select air fry mode, then set the temperature to 400 °F and timer for 10 minutes. Turn lamb chops halfway through.
5. Serve and enjoy.

Nutrition: Calories: 266 Fat: 11 g Protein: 38 g Carbs: 0.5 g Fiber: 3.8 g Sugars: 0g Sodium: 463 mg

Poultry

– RECIPES –

Asian Chicken Stir-Fry

Preparation time: 10 minutes

Cooking time: 10 minutes

Servings: 4

Ingredients:

> 3 tablespoons extra-virgin olive oil
> 1 pound (454 g) chicken breasts or thighs, cut into ¾-inch pieces
> 2 cups edamame or pea pods
> 3 garlic cloves, chopped
> 1 tablespoon peeled and grated fresh ginger
> 2 tablespoons reduced-sodium soy sauce
> Juice of 2 limes
> 1 teaspoon sesame oil
> 2 teaspoons toasted sesame seeds
> 1 tablespoon chopped fresh cilantro

Direction:

1. In a large skillet over medium-high heat, heat the olive oil until it shimmers. Add the chicken to the oil and cook, occasionally stirring, until opaque, about 5 minutes. Add the edamame and cook, occasionally stirring, until crisp-tender, 3 to 5 minutes. Add the garlic and ginger and cook, constantly stirring, for 30 seconds.
2. In a small bowl, whisk together the soy sauce, lime juice, and sesame oil. Add the sauce mixture to the pan. Bring to a simmer, stirring, and cook for 2 minutes.
3. Remove from heat and garnish with the sesame seeds and cilantro.

Nutrition: Calories: 331 Fat: 17 g Protein: 31 g
Carbs: 11 g Fiber: 5 g Sugars: 0 g Sodium: 342 mg

Bacon and Chicken Garlic Wrap

Preparation time: 15 minutes

Cooking time: 10 minutes

Servings: 2

Ingredients:

> 1 chicken fillet, cut into small cubes
> 8-9 thin slices of bacon, cut to fit cubes
> 6 garlic cloves, minced

Directions:

1. Pre-heat your oven to 400 °F. Line a baking tray with aluminum foil.
2. Add minced garlic to a bowl and rub each chicken piece with it. Wrap a bacon piece around each garlic chicken bite.
3. Secure with a toothpick. Transfer bites to a baking sheet, keeping a little bit of space between them.
4. Bake for about 15-20 minutes until crispy. Serve and enjoy!

Nutrition: Calories: 260 Fats: 19 g Proteins: 22 g
Carbs: 5 g Fiber: 4.8 g Sugar: 21 g Sodium: 351 mg

Baked Turkey Spaghetti

Preparation time: 5 minutes

Cooking time: 20 minutes

Servings: 2

Ingredients:

> 1 (10-ounce / 283-g) package zucchini noodles
> 2 tablespoons extra-virgin olive oil, divided
> 1 pound (454 g) 93% lean ground turkey
> 1/2 teaspoon dried oregano
> 2 cups low-sodium spaghetti sauce
> 1/2 cup shredded sharp Cheddar cheese

Directions:

1. Pat zucchini noodles dry between two paper towels.
2. In an oven-safe medium skillet, heat 1 tablespoon of olive oil over medium heat. When hot, add the zucchini noodles. Cook for 3 minutes, stirring halfway through.
3. Add the remaining 1 tablespoon of oil, ground turkey, and oregano. Cook for 7 to 10 minutes, stirring and breaking apart as needed. Add the spaghetti sauce to the skillet and stir.
4. If your broiler is on the top of your oven, place the oven rack in the center position. Set the broiler on high. Top the mixture with the cheese, and broil for 5 minutes or until the cheese is bubbly.

Nutrition: Calories: 335 Fat: 21 g Protein: 28 g Carbs: 12 g Fibers: 3 g Sugars: 4 g Sodium: 216 mg

Blackened Chicken Bake

Preparation time: 10 minutes

Cooking time: 18 minutes

Servings: 2

Ingredients:

> 4 chicken breasts
> 2 teaspoon olive oil

Seasoning:

> 1 1/2 tablespoon brown sugar
> 1 teaspoon paprika
> 1 teaspoon dried oregano
> 1/4 teaspoon garlic powder
> 1/2 teaspoon salt and pepper

Garnish:

> Chopped parsley

Directions:

1. Mix olive oil with brown sugar, paprika, oregano, garlic powder, salt, and black pepper in a bowl. Place the chicken breasts in the baking tray of the Oven.
2. Pour and rub this mixture liberally over all the chicken breasts. Turn the dial to select the "Bake" mode.
3. Hit the Time button and again use the dial to set the cooking time to 18 minutes. Now push the Temp button and rotate the dial to set the temperature at 425 °F.
4. Once preheated, place the baking tray inside the oven. Serve warm.

Nutrition: Calories: 412 Fats: 25 g Proteins: 19 g Carbs: 44 g Fiber: 2.5 g Sugar: 14 g Sodium: 357 mg

Chicken Caesar Salad

Preparation time: 10 minutes

Cooking time: 15 minutes

Servings: 2

Ingredients:

> 1 garlic clove
> ½ teaspoon anchovy paste
> Juice of ½ lemon
> 2 tablespoons extra-virgin olive oil
> 1 (8-ounce / 227-g) boneless, skinless chicken breast
> ¼ teaspoon salt
> Freshly ground black pepper, to taste
> 2 romaine lettuce hearts, cored and chopped
> 1 red bell pepper, seeded and cut into thin strips
> ¼ cup grated Parmesan cheese

Direction:

1. Preheat the broiler to high. In a blender jar, combine the garlic, anchovy paste, lemon juice, and olive oil. Process until smooth and set aside.
2. Cut the chicken breast lengthwise into two even cutlets of similar thickness. Season the chicken with salt and pepper, and place it on a baking sheet.
3. Broil the chicken for 5 to 7 minutes on each side until cooked through and browned. Cut into thin strips.
4. In a medium mixing bowl, toss the lettuce, bell pepper, and cheese. Add the dressing and toss to coat. Divide the salad between 2 plates and top with the chicken.

Nutrition: Calories: 292 Fat: 18 g Protein: 28 g
Carbs: 6 g Fiber: 2 g Sugars: 3 g Sodium: 706 mg

Chicken in Wine

Preparation time: 10 minutes

Cooking time: 12 minutes

Servings: 2

Ingredients:

> 2 pounds (907 g) of chicken breasts, trimmed of skin and fat
> 1 (10¾-ounce / 305-g) can 98% fat-free, reduced-sodium cream of mushroom soup
> 1 (10¾-ounce / 305-g) can of French onion soup
> 1 cup dry white wine or chicken broth

Direction:

1. Place the chicken into the Instant Pot.
2. Combine soups and wine. Pour over chicken.
3. Secure the lid and make sure the vent is set to sealing. Cook on Manual mode for 12 minutes.
4. When cook time is up, let the pressure release naturally for 5 minutes and then release the rest manually.

Nutrition: Calories: 225 Fat: 5 g Protein: 35 g
Carbs: 7 g Fiber: 1 g Sugars: 3 g Sodium: 645 mg

Chicken Romaine Salad

Preparation time: 15 minutes
Cooking time: 0 minutes
Servings: 2
Ingredients:

> 2 cups shredded rotisserie chicken
> 11/2 tablespoons plain low-fat Greek yogurt
> 1/8 teaspoon freshly ground black pepper
> 1/4 cup halved purple seedless grapes
> 8 cups chopped romaine lettuce
> 1 medium tomato, sliced
> 1 avocado, sliced

Directions:

1. In a large bowl, combine the chicken, yogurt, and pepper, and mix well.
2. Stir in the grapes.
3. Divide the lettuce into four portions. Spoon one-quarter of the chicken salad onto each portion and top with a couple of slices of tomato and avocado.

Nutrition: Calories: 203 Fats: 5 g Proteins: 22 g
Carbs: 10 g Fibers: 5 g Sugars: 4 g Sodium: 56 mg

Greek Chicken

Preparation time: 25 minutes
Cooking time: 20 minutes
Servings: 2
Ingredients:

> 4 potatoes, unpeeled, quartered
> 2 pounds (907 g) of chicken pieces, trimmed of skin and fat
> 2 large onions, quartered
> 1 whole bulb garlic, cloves minced
> 3 teaspoons dried oregano
> ¾ teaspoons salt
> ½ teaspoon pepper
> 1 tablespoon olive oil
> 1 cup water

Direction:

1. Place potatoes, chicken, onions, and garlic into the inner pot of the Instant Pot, then sprinkle with seasonings. Top with oil and water.
2. Secure the lid and make sure the vent is set to sealing. Cook on Manual mode for 20 minutes.
3. When cook time is over, let the pressure release naturally for 5 minutes, then release the rest manually.

Nutrition: Calories: 278 Fat: 6 g Protein: 27 g
Carbs: 29 g Fiber: 4 g Sugars: 9 g Sodium: 358 mg

Grilled Lime Chicken

Preparation time: 10 minutes

Cooking time: 25 minutes

Servings: 2

Ingredients

> 8 boneless skinless chicken breast halves (4 oz. each)
> 1/2 cup lime juice
> 1/3 cup olive oil
> 4 green onions, chopped
> 4 garlic cloves, minced
> 3 tbsps. Chopped fresh dill, divided
> 1/4 tsp. pepper

Direction:

1. Flatten the chicken breasts into 1/4-inch. Mix together the 2 tbsp. Pepper and dill, garlic, onions, oil and lime juice in a resealable plastic bag, then add the chicken. Seal the bag securely and flip to coat, then let it chill in the fridge for 2-4 hours.
2. Drain and get rid of the marinade. Grill the chicken for 6-7 minutes per side on medium-hot heat without a cover or until a thermometer reads 170 °F. Sprinkle the leftover dill on top.

Nutrition: Calories: 235 Fat: 12 g Protein: 27 g
Carbs: 3 g Fiber: 3.6 g Sugar: 14 g Sodium: 66 mg

Ground Chicken Meatballs

Preparation time: 10 minutes

Cooking time: 10 minutes

Servings: 2

Ingredients:

> 1-lb. ground chicken
> 1/3 cup panko
> 1 teaspoon salt
> 2 teaspoons chives
> 1/2 teaspoon garlic powder
> 1 teaspoon thyme
> 1 egg

Directions:

1. Toss all the meatball ingredients in a bowl and mix well. Make small meatballs out of this mixture and place them in the air fryer basket.
2. Press the "Power Button" of the Air Fry Oven and turn the dial to select the "Air Fry" mode. Press the Time button and again turn the dial to set the cooking time to 10 minutes.
3. Now push the Temp button and rotate the dial to set the temperature at 350 °F. Once preheated, place the air fryer basket inside and close its lid. Serve warm.

Nutrition: Calories: 453 Fats: 2 g Proteins: 23 g
Carbs: 18 g Fiber: 2.6 g Sugar: 13 g Sodium: 521 mg

One-Pan Chicken Dinner

Preparation time: 5 minutes

Cooking time: 35 minutes

Servings: 2

Ingredients:

> 3 tablespoons extra-virgin olive oil
> 1 tablespoon red wine vinegar or apple cider vinegar
> 1/4 teaspoon garlic powder
> 3 tablespoons Italian seasoning
> 4 (4-ounce / 113-g) boneless, skinless chicken breasts
> 2 cups cubed sweet potatoes
> 20 Brussels sprouts, halved lengthwise

Directions:

1. Preheat the oven to 400 °F (205 °C).
2. In a large bowl, whisk together the oil, vinegar, garlic powder, and Italian seasoning. Add the chicken, sweet potatoes, and Brussels sprouts, and coat thoroughly with the marinade.
3. Remove the ingredients from the marinade and arrange them on a baking sheet in a single layer. Roast for 15 minutes.
4. Remove the baking sheet from the oven, flip the chicken over, and bake for another 15 to 20 minutes.

Nutrition: Calories: 342 Fat: 16 g Protein: 30 g Carbs: 23 g Fibers: 9 g Sugars: 8 g Sodium: 186 mg

Orange Chicken

Preparation time: 10 minutes

Cooking time: 10 minutes

Servings: 4

Ingredients:

> 3 tablespoons extra-virgin olive oil
> 1 pound (454 g) chicken breasts or thighs, cut into ¾-inch pieces
> 1 teaspoon peeled and grated fresh ginger
> 2 garlic cloves, minced
> 1 tablespoon honey
> Juice and zest of 1 orange
> 1 teaspoon cornstarch
> ½ teaspoon sriracha (or to taste)
> Sesame seeds (optional, for garnish)
> Thinly sliced scallion (optional, for garnish)

Direction:

1. In a large skillet over medium-high heat, heat the olive oil until it shimmers. Add the chicken to the oil and cook, occasionally stirring, until opaque, about 5 minutes. Add the ginger and garlic and cook, constantly stirring, for 30 seconds.
2. In a small bowl, whisk together the honey, orange juice and zest, cornstarch, and sriracha. Add the sauce mixture to the chicken and cook, stirring, until the sauce thickens, about 2 minutes.
3. Serve garnished with sesame seeds and sliced scallions, if desired.

Nutrition: Calories: 245 Fat: 12 g Protein: 26 g Carbs: 9 g Fiber: 0 g Sugars: 4 g Sodium: 75 mg

Oregano Chicken Breast

Preparation time: 10 minutes

Cooking time: 25 minutes

Servings: 2

Ingredients:

> 2 lbs. chicken breasts, minced
> 1 tablespoon avocado oil
> 1 teaspoon smoked paprika
> 1 teaspoon garlic powder
> 1 teaspoon oregano
> 1/2 teaspoon salt
> Black pepper, to taste

Directions:

1. Toss all the meatball ingredients in a bowl and mix well. Make small meatballs out of this mixture and place them in the air fryer basket.
2. Press the "Power Button" of the Air Fry Oven and turn the dial to select the "Air Fry" mode. Press the Time button and again turn the dial to set the cooking time to 25 minutes
3. Now push the Temp button and rotate the dial to set the temperature at 375 °F. Once preheated, place the air fryer basket inside and close its lid. Serve warm.

Nutrition: Calories: 352 Fat: 14 g Protein: 26 g
Carbs: 16 g Fiber: 3.7 g Sugar: 165 g Sodium: 235 mg

Peppered Chicken with Balsamic Kale

Preparation time: 5 minutes

Cooking time: 15 minutes

Servings: 2

Ingredients:

> 4 (4-ounce / 113-g) boneless, skinless chicken breasts
> 1/4 teaspoon salt
> 1 tablespoon freshly ground black pepper
> 2 tablespoons unsalted butter
> 1 tablespoon extra-virgin olive oil
> 8 cups stemmed and roughly chopped kale, loosely packed (about 2 bunches)
> 1/2 cup balsamic vinegar
> 20 cherry tomatoes, halved

Directions:

1. Season both sides of the chicken breasts with salt and pepper.
2. Heat a large skillet over medium heat. When hot, heat the butter and oil. Add the chicken and cook for 8 to 10 minutes, flipping halfway through. When cooked all the way through, remove the chicken from the skillet and set it aside.
3. Increase the heat to medium-high. Put the kale in the skillet and cook for 3 minutes, stirring every minute. Add the vinegar and the tomatoes and cook for another 3 to 5 minutes.
4. Divide the kale and tomato mixture into four equal portions, and top each portion with 1 chicken breast.

Nutrition: Calories: 293 Fat: 11 g Protein: 31 g
Carbs: 18 g Fibers: 3 g Sugars: 4 g Sodium: 328 mg

Saffron Chicken

Preparation time: 10 minutes
Cooking time: 10 minutes
Servings: 4
Ingredients:

> Pinch saffron (3 or 4 threads)
> ½ cup plain nonfat yogurt
> 2 tablespoons water
> ½ onion, chopped
> 3 garlic cloves, minced
> 2 tablespoons chopped fresh cilantro
> Juice of ½ lemon
> ½ teaspoon salt
> 1 pound (454 g) boneless, skinless chicken breasts, cut into 2-inch strips
> 1 tablespoon extra-virgin olive oil

Direction:

1. In a blender jar, combine the saffron, yogurt, water, onion, garlic, cilantro, lemon juice, and salt. Pulse to blend.
2. In a large mixing bowl, combine the chicken and the yogurt sauce, and stir to coat. Cover and refrigerate for at least 1 hour or up to overnight.
3. In a large skillet, heat the oil over medium heat. Add the chicken pieces, shaking off any excess marinade. Discard the marinade. Cook the chicken pieces on each side for 5 minutes, flipping once until cooked through and golden brown.

Nutrition: Calories: 155 Fat: 5 g Protein: 26 g
Carbs: 3 g Fiber: 0 g Sugars: 1 g Sodium: 501 mg

Savory Rubbed Roast Chicken

Preparation time: 10 minutes
Cooking time: 35 minutes
Servings: 6
Ingredients:

> 1 teaspoon ground paprika
> 1 teaspoon garlic powder
> ½ teaspoon ground coriander
> ½ teaspoon ground cumin
> ½ teaspoon salt
> ¼ teaspoon ground cayenne pepper
> 4 chicken legs
> 1 teaspoon extra-virgin olive oil

Direction:

1. Preheat the oven to 400°F (205°C).
2. In a small bowl, combine the paprika, garlic powder, coriander, cumin, salt, and cayenne pepper. Rub the chicken legs all over with the spices.
3. In an ovenproof skillet, heat the oil over medium heat. Sear the chicken for 8 to 10 minutes on each side until the skin browns and becomes crisp.
4. Transfer the skillet to the oven and continue to cook for 10 to 15 minutes until the chicken is cooked through and its juices run clear.

Nutrition: Calories: 276 Fat: 16 g Protein: 30 g
Carbs: 1 g Fiber: 0 g Sugars: 0 g Sodium: 256 mg

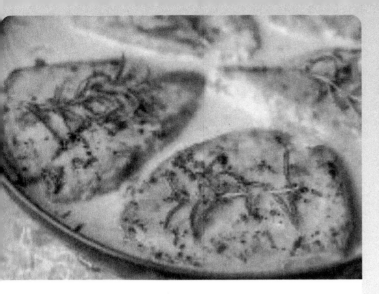

Smothered Dijon Chicken

Preparation time: 10 minutes

Cooking time: 30 minutes

Servings: 4

Ingredients:

- ¾ cup low-fat buttermilk
- 2 tablespoons Dijon mustard
- 3 garlic cloves, minced
- 1 tablespoon dried dill
- 1 teaspoon mustard seeds
- 2 boneless, skinless chicken breasts
- 2 large carrots, peeled and halved
- 1 medium onion, quartered

Direction:

1. Preheat the oven to 375°F (190°C). In a medium bowl, combine the buttermilk, mustard, garlic, dill, and mustard seeds. Mix well.
2. Add the chicken, carrots, and onion, coating them thoroughly with the buttermilk mixture. Set aside to marinate for at least 15 minutes.
3. Place the chicken, carrots, and onions on a rimmed baking sheet. Discard the remaining buttermilk mixture.
4. Transfer the baking sheet to the oven, and bake for 30 minutes, or until the vegetables are tender, the chicken is cooked through, and its juices run clear. Serve warm and enjoy.

Nutrition: Calories: 119 Fat: 2 g Protein: 16 g
Carbs: 10 g Fiber: 2 g Sugars: 5 g Sodium: 202 mg

Teriyaki Meatballs

Preparation time: 20 minutes

Cooking time: 20 minutes

Servings: 6

Ingredients:

- 1 pound (454 g) lean ground turkey
- ¼ cup finely chopped scallions, both white and green parts
- 1 egg
- 2 garlic cloves, minced
- 1 teaspoon grated fresh ginger
- 2 tablespoons reduced-sodium tamari or gluten-free soy sauce
- 1 tablespoon honey
- 2 teaspoons mirin
- 1 teaspoon toasted sesame oil

Direction:

1. Preheat the oven to 400°F (205°C). Line a baking sheet with parchment paper.
2. In a large mixing bowl, combine the turkey, scallions, egg, garlic, ginger, tamari, honey, mirin, and sesame oil. Mix well.
3. Using your hands, form the meat mixture into balls about the size of a tablespoon. Arrange on the prepared baking sheet.
4. Bake for 10 minutes, flip with a spatula and continue baking for an additional 10 minutes until the meatballs are cooked through.

Nutrition: Calories: 153 Fat: 8 g Protein: 16 g
Carbs: 5 g Fiber: 0 g Sugars: 4 g Sodium: 270 mg

Turkey Chili

Preparation time: 15 minutes

Cooking time: 30 minutes

Servings: 6

Ingredients:

> 1 tablespoon extra-virgin olive oil
> 1 pound (454 g) lean ground turkey
> 1 large onion, diced
> 3 garlic cloves, minced
> 1 red bell pepper, seeded and diced
> 1 cup chopped celery
> 2 tablespoons chili powder
> 1 tablespoon ground cumin
> 1 (28-ounce / 794-g) can of reduced-salt diced tomatoes
> 1 (15-ounce / 425-g) can of low-sodium kidney beans, drained and rinsed
> 2 cups low-sodium chicken broth
> ½ teaspoon salt
> Shredded Cheddar cheese for serving (optional)

Direction:

1. In a large pot, heat the oil over medium heat. Add the turkey, onion, and garlic, and cook, stirring regularly, until the turkey is cooked through.
2. Add the bell pepper, celery, chili powder, and cumin. Stir well and continue to cook for 1 minute.
3. Add the tomatoes with their liquid, kidney beans, and chicken broth. Bring to a boil, reduce the heat to low, and simmer for 20 minutes.
4. Season with the salt and serve topped with cheese (if using).

Nutrition: Calories: 276 Fat: 10 g Protein: 23 g Carbs: 27 g Fiber: 8 g Sugars: 7 g Sodium: 556 mg

Turkey Meatballs

Preparation time: 10 minutes

Cooking time: 20 minutes

Servings: 2

Ingredients:

> 1 lb. turkey mince
> 1 red bell pepper, deseeded and chopped
> 1 large egg, beaten
> 4 tablespoons parsley, minced
> 1 tablespoon cilantro, minced
> Salt, to taste
> Black pepper, to taste

Directions:

1. Toss all the meatball ingredients in a bowl and mix well. Make small meatballs out of this mixture and place them in the air fryer basket.
2. Press the "Power Button" of the Air Fry Oven and turn the dial to select the "Air Fry" mode. Press the Time button and again turn the dial to set the cooking time to 20 minutes
3. Now push the Temp button and rotate the dial to set the temperature at 375 °F. Once preheated, place the air fryer basket inside and close its lid. Serve warm.

Nutrition: Calories: 338 Fat: 10 g Protein: 10 g Carbs: 32 g Fiber: 3.7 g Sugars: 24 g Sodium: 432 mg

Fish And Seafood

– RECIPES –

Baked Salmon with Garlic Parmesan Topping

Preparation time: 10 minutes

Cooking time: 30 minutes

Servings: 2

Ingredients:

> 1 lb. wild-caught salmon filets
> 2 tbsp. margarine

What you'll need from the store cupboard:

> ¼ cup reduced-fat parmesan cheese, grated
> ¼ cup light mayonnaise
> 2-3 cloves garlic, diced
> 2 tbsp. parsley
> Salt and pepper to taste

Directions:

1. Heat the oven to 350 and line a baking pan with parchment paper. Place salmon on pan and season with salt and pepper.
2. In a medium skillet, over medium heat, melt butter. Add garlic and cook, stirring 1 minute.
3. Reduce heat to low and add remaining ingredients. Stir until everything is melted and combined.
4. Spread evenly over salmon and bake for 15 minutes for thawed fish or 20 for frozen. Salmon is done when it flakes easily with a fork. Serve.

Nutrition: Calories: 408 Fat: 24 g Protein: 41 g Carbs: 4 g Fiber: 0 g Sugar: 1 g Sodium: 387 mg

Cajun Catfish

Preparation time: 10 minutes

Cooking time: 30 minutes

Servings: 2

Ingredients:

> 4 (8 oz.) catfish fillets

What you'll need from the store cupboard:

> 2 tbsp. olive oil
> 2 tsp garlic salt
> 2 tsp thyme
> 2 tsp paprika
> ½ tsp cayenne pepper
> ½ tsp red hot sauce
> ¼ tsp black pepper
> Nonstick cooking spray

Directions:

1. Heat oven to 450 degrees. Spray a 9x13-inch baking dish with cooking spray.
2. In a small bowl, whisk together everything but catfish. Brush both sides of fillets, using all the spice mix.
3. Bake 10-13 minutes or until fish flakes easily with a fork. Serve.

Nutrition: Calories: 366 Fat: 24 g Protein: 35 g Carbs: 0 g Fiber: 0 g Sugar: 0 g Sodium: 123 mg

Cajun Shrimp and Roasted Vegetables

Preparation time: 5 minutes

Cooking time: 15 minutes

Servings: 2

Ingredients:

> 1 lb. large shrimp, peeled and deveined
> 2 zucchinis, sliced
> 2 yellow squashes, sliced
> 1/2 bunch asparagus, cut into thirds
> 2 red bell pepper, cut into chunks

What you'll need from the store cupboard:

> 2 tbsp. olive oil
> 2 tbsp. Cajun Seasoning
> Salt and pepper to taste

Directions:

1. Heat oven to 400 degrees.
2. Combine shrimp and vegetables in a large bowl. Add oil and seasoning and toss to coat.
3. Spread evenly on a large baking sheet and bake for 15-20 minutes, or until vegetables are tender. Serve.

Nutrition: Calories: 251 Fat: 9 g Protein: 30 g Carbs: 13 g Fiber: 4 g Sugar: 6 g Sodium: 213 mg

Cilantro Lime Grilled Shrimp

Preparation time: 5 minutes

Cooking time: 5 minutes

Servings: 2

Ingredients:

> 1 1/2 lbs. large shrimp raw, peeled, deveined with tails on
> Juice and zest of 1 lime
> 2 tbsp. fresh cilantro chopped

What you'll need from the store cupboard:

> ¼ cup olive oil
> 2 cloves garlic, diced fine
> 1 tsp. Smoked paprika
> ¼ tsp. cumin
> 1/2 teaspoon salt
> ¼ tsp. cayenne pepper

Directions:

1. Place the shrimp in a large Ziploc bag.
2. Mix remaining ingredients in a small bowl and pour over shrimp. Let marinate for 20-30 minutes.
3. Heat up the grill. Skewer the shrimp and cook 2-3 minutes per side, just until they turn to pick. Be careful not to overcook them. Serve garnished with cilantro.

Nutrition: Calories: 317 Fat: 15 g Protein: 39 g Carbs: 4g Fiber: 0 g Sugar: 0 g Sodium: 432 mg

Cioppino

Preparation time: 10 minutes

Cooking time: 20 minutes

Servings: 4

Ingredients:

> 2 tablespoons extra-virgin olive oil
> 1 onion, finely chopped
> 1 garlic clove, minced
> ½ cup dry white wine
> 1 (14-ounce / 397-g) can tomato sauce
> 8 ounces (227 g) cod, pin bones removed, cut into 1-inch pieces
> 8 ounces (227 g) shrimp, peeled and deveined
> 1 tablespoon Italian seasoning
> ½ teaspoon sea salt
> Pinch red pepper flakes

Direction:

1. In a large skillet over medium-high heat, heat the olive oil until it shimmers. Add the onion and cook, occasionally stirring, for 3 minutes. Add the garlic and cook, constantly stirring, for 30 seconds. Add the wine and cook, stirring, for 1 minute.
2. Add the tomato sauce. Bring to a simmer. Stir in the cod, shrimp, Italian seasoning, salt, and pepper flakes. Simmer until the fish is just opaque, about 5 minutes.

Nutrition: Calories: 243 Fat: 8 g Protein: 23 g Carbs: 11 g Fiber: 2 g Sugars: 7 g Sodium: 271 mg

Cod with Mango Salsa

Preparation time: 10 minutes

Cooking time: 10 minutes

Servings: 4

Ingredients:

> 1 pound (454 g) cod, cut into 4 fillets, pin bones removed
> 2 tablespoons extra-virgin olive oil
> ¾ teaspoon sea salt, divided
> 1 mango, pitted, peeled, and cut into cubes
> ¼ cup chopped cilantro
> ½ red onion, finely chopped
> 1 jalapeño, seeded and finely chopped
> 1 garlic clove, minced
> Juice of 1 lime

Direction:

1. Preheat the oven broiler to high.
2. On a rimmed baking sheet, brush the cod with olive oil and season with ½ teaspoon of salt. Broil until the fish is opaque, 5 to 10 minutes.
3. Meanwhile, in a small bowl, combine the mango, cilantro, onion, jalapeño, garlic, lime juice, and remaining ¼ teaspoon of salt.
4. Serve the cod with the salsa spooned over the top.

Nutrition: Calories: 197 Fat: 8 g Protein: 21 g Carbs: 13 g Fiber: 2 g Sugars: 12 g Sodium: 354 mg

Crab Frittata

Preparation time: 10 minutes

Cooking time: 50 minutes

Servings: 2

Ingredients:

> 4 eggs
> 2 cups lump crabmeat
> 1 cup half-n-half
> 1 cup green onions, diced

What you'll need from the store cupboard:

> 1 cup reduced-fat parmesan cheese, grated
> 1 tsp. salt
> 1 tsp. pepper
> 1 tsp. smoked paprika
> 1 tsp. Italian seasoning
> Nonstick cooking spray

Directions:

1. Heat oven to 350 degrees. Spray an 8-inch springform pan or pie plate with cooking spray.
2. In a large bowl, whisk together the eggs and half-n-half. Add seasonings and parmesan cheese, and stir to mix.
3. Stir in the onions and crab meat. Pour into prepared pan and bake 35-40 minutes, or eggs are set and the top is lightly browned.
4. Let cool for 10 minutes, then slice and serve warm or at room temperature.

Nutrition: Calories: 276 Fat: 17 g Protein: 25 g Carbs: 5 g Fiber: 1 g Sugar: 1 g Sodium: 135 mg

Crunchy Lemon Shrimp

Preparation time: 5 minutes

Cooking time: 10 minutes

Servings: 2

Ingredients:

> 1 lb. raw shrimp, peeled and deveined
> 2 tbsp. Italian parsley, roughly chopped
> 2 tbsp. lemon juice, divided

What you'll need from the store cupboard:

> 2/3 cup panko bread crumbs
> 2 1/2 tbsp. olive oil, divided
> Salt and pepper to taste

Directions:

1. Heat oven to 400 degrees.
2. Place the shrimp evenly in a baking dish and sprinkle with salt and pepper. Drizzle on 1 tablespoon lemon juice and 1 tablespoon of olive oil. Set aside.
3. In a medium bowl, combine parsley, remaining lemon juice, bread crumbs, remaining olive oil, and ¼ tsp. Each of salt and pepper. Layer the panko mixture evenly on top of the shrimp.
4. Bake 8-10 minutes or until shrimp are cooked through and the panko is golden brown.

Nutrition: Calories: 283 Fat: 12 g Protein: 28 g Carbs: 15 g Fiber: 1 g Sugar: 1 g Sodium: 93 mg

Curried Tuna Salad Lettuce Wraps

Preparation time: 10 minutes

Cooking time: 0 minutes

Servings: 2

Ingredients:

> 1/3 cup mayonnaise
> 1 tablespoon freshly squeezed lemon juice
> 1 teaspoon curry powder
> 1 teaspoon reduced-sodium soy sauce
> ½ teaspoon sriracha (or to taste)
> ½ cup canned water chestnuts, drained and chopped
> 2 (2.6-ounce / 74-g) packages of tuna packed in water, drained
> Two large butter lettuce leaves

Direction:

1. In a medium bowl, whisk together the mayonnaise, lemon juice, curry powder, soy sauce, and sriracha.
2. Add the water chestnuts and tuna. Stir to combine.
3. Serve wrapped in the lettuce leaves.

Nutrition: Calories: 271 Fat: 14 g Protein: 19 g
Carbs: 18 g Fiber: 3 g Sugars: 1 g Sodium: 627 mg

Easy Salmon Stew

Preparation time: 10 minutes

Cooking time: 30 minutes

Servings: 2

Ingredients:

> 2 lbs. salmon fillet, cubed
> 1 onion, chopped
> 2 cups fish broth
> 1 tbsp olive oil
> Pepper to taste
> salt to taste

Directions:

1. Add oil into the inner pot of the instant pot and set the pot on sauté mode.
2. Add onion and sauté for 2 minutes. Add remaining ingredients and stir well.
3. Seal pot with lid and cook on high for 6 minutes.
4. Once done, release pressure using quick release. Remove lid. Stir and serve.

Nutrition: Calories: 243 Fat: 12.6 g Protein: 31 g
Carbs: 0.8 g Fiber: 3.2 g Sugar: 0.3 g Sodium: 421 mg

Fish with Mushrooms

Preparation time: 5 minutes

Cooking time: 16 minutes

Servings: 2

Ingredients:

> 1-pound cod fillet
> 2 tablespoons butter
> ¼ cup white onion, chopped
> 1 cup fresh mushrooms
> 1 teaspoon dried thyme

Directions:

1. Put the fish in a baking pan. Preheat your oven to 450 degrees F.
2. Melt the butter and cook the onion and mushroom for 1 minute.
3. Spread mushroom mixture on top of the fish. Season with thyme.
4. Bake in the oven for 15 minutes.

Nutrition: Calories: 156 Fat: 7 g Protein: 21 g Carbs: 3 g Fiber: 0.5 g Sugar:13 g Sodium: 110 mg

Grilled Tuna Steaks

Preparation time: 5 minutes

Cooking time: 10 minutes

Servings: 2

Ingredients:

> 6 oz. tuna steaks
> 3 tbsp. fresh basil, diced

What you'll need from the store cupboard:

> 4 1/2tsp. Olive oil
> ¾ tsp. Salt
> ¼ tsp. pepper
> Nonstick cooking spray

Directions:

1. Heat grill to medium heat. Spray rack with cooking spray.
2. Drizzle both sides of the tuna with oil. Sprinkle with basil, salt and pepper.
3. Place on grill and cook 5 minutes per side, tuna should be slightly pink in the center. Serve.

Nutrition: Calories: 343 Fat: 14 g Protein: 51 g Carbs: 0 g Fiber: 0 g Sugar: 0 g Sodium: 356 mg

Honey Mustard Roasted Salmon

Preparation time: 5 minutes

Cooking time: 20 minutes

Servings: 4

Ingredients:

> Nonstick cooking spray
> 2 tablespoons whole-grain mustard
> 1 tablespoon honey
> 2 garlic cloves, minced
> ¼ teaspoon salt
> ¼ teaspoon freshly ground black pepper
> 1 pound (454 g) salmon fillet

Direction:

1. Preheat the oven to 425°F (220°C). Spray a baking sheet with nonstick cooking spray.
2. In a small bowl, whisk together the mustard, honey, garlic, salt, and pepper.
3. Place the salmon fillet on the prepared baking sheet, skin-side down. Spoon the sauce onto the salmon and spread evenly.
4. Roast for 15 to 20 minutes, depending on the thickness of the fillet until the flesh flakes easily.

Nutrition: Calories: 186 Fat: 7 g Protein: 23 g Carbs: 6 g Fiber: 0 g Sugars: 4 g Sodium: 312 mg

Lemon Pepper Salmon

Preparation time: 5 minutes

Cooking time: 20 minutes

Servings: 2

Ingredients:

> Nonstick cooking spray
> ½ teaspoon freshly ground black pepper
> ¼ teaspoon salt
> Zest and juice of ½ lemon
> ¼ teaspoon dried thyme
> 1 pound (454 g) salmon fillet

Direction:

1. Preheat the oven to 425°F (220°C). Spray a baking sheet with nonstick cooking spray.
2. In a small bowl, combine the pepper, salt, lemon zest and juice, and thyme. Stir to combine.
3. Place the salmon on the prepared baking sheet, skin-side down. Spread the seasoning mixture evenly over the fillet.
4. Bake for 15 to 20 minutes, depending on the thickness of the fillet until the flesh flakes easily.

Nutrition: Calories: 163 Fat: 7 g Protein: 23 g Carbs: 1 g Fiber: 0 g Sugars: 0 g Sodium: 167 mg

Open-Faced Tuna Melts

Preparation time: 5 minutes

Cooking time: 5 minutes

Servings: 3

Ingredients:

> 3 English muffins, 100% whole-wheat
> 2 (5-ounce / 142-g) cans chunk-light tuna, drained
> 3 tablespoons plain low-fat Greek yogurt
> ½ teaspoon freshly ground black pepper
> ¾ cup shredded Cheddar cheese

Direction:

1. If your broiler is on the top of your oven, place the oven rack in the center position. Turn the broiler on high.
2. Split the English muffins, if necessary, and toast them in the toaster.
3. Meanwhile, in a medium bowl, mix the tuna, yogurt, and pepper.
4. Place the muffin halves on a baking sheet, and spoon one-sixth of the tuna mixture and 2 tablespoons of Cheddar cheese on top of each half. Broil for 2 minutes or until the cheese melts.

Nutrition: Calories: 392 Fat: 13 g Protein: 40 g

Carbs: 28 g Fiber: 5 g Sugars: 6 g Sodium: 474 mg

Red Clam Sauce and Pasta

Preparation time: 10 minutes

Cooking time: 3 hours

Servings: 2

Ingredients:

> 1 onion, diced
> ¼ cup fresh parsley, diced

What you'll need from the store cupboard:

> 2 6 1/2 oz. cans clams, chopped, undrained
> 14 1/2 oz. tomatoes, diced, undrained
> 6 oz. tomato paste
> 2 cloves garlic, diced
> 1 bay leaf
> 1 tbsp. sunflower oil
> 1 tsp. Splenda
> 1 tsp. Basil
> ½ tsp. thyme
> 1/2 Homemade Pasta, cook & drain

Directions:

1. Heat oil in a small skillet over med-high heat. Add onion and cook until tender; add garlic and cook 1 minute more. Transfer to crock pot.
2. Add remaining ingredients, except pasta, cover and cook on low for 3-4 hours.
3. Discard bay leaf and serve over cooked pasta.

Nutrition: Calories: 223 Fat: 6 g Protein: 12 g

Carbs: 32 g Fiber: 5 g Sugar: 15 g Sodium: 571 mg

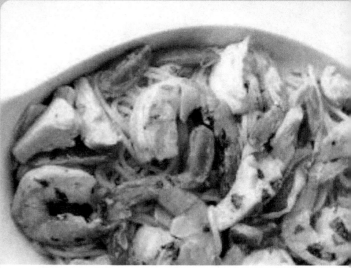

Salmon Milano

Preparation time: 10 minutes

Cooking time: 20 minutes

Servings: 2

Ingredients:

> 2 1/2 lb. salmon filet
> 2 tomatoes, sliced
> 1/2 cup margarine

What you'll need from the store cupboard:

> 1/2 cup basil pesto

Directions:

1. Heat the oven to 400 degrees. Line a 9x15-inch baking sheet with foil, making sure it covers the sides. Place another large piece of foil onto the baking sheet and place the salmon filet on top of it.
2. Place the pesto and margarine in a blender or food processor and pulse until smooth. Spread evenly over salmon. Place tomato slices on top.
3. Wrap the foil around the salmon, tenting around the top to prevent foil from touching the salmon as much as possible. Bake 15-25 minutes, or salmon flakes easily with a fork. Serve.

Nutrition: Calories: 444 Fat: 24 g Protein: 55 g Carbs: 2 g Fiber: 0 g Sugar: 1 g Sodium: 388 mg

Shrimp and Artichoke Skillet

Preparation time: 5 minutes

Cooking time: 10 minutes

Servings: 2

Ingredients:

> 1 1/2 cups shrimp, peel & devein
> 2 shallots, diced
> 1 tbsp. margarine

What you'll need from the store cupboard

> 2 12 oz. jars artichoke hearts, drain & rinse
> 2 cups white wine
> 2 cloves garlic, diced fine

Directions:

1. Melt margarine in a large skillet over med-high heat. Add shallot and garlic and cook until they start to brown, stirring frequently.
2. Add artichokes and cook for 5 minutes. Reduce heat and add wine. Cook for 3 minutes, stirring occasionally.
3. Add the shrimp and cook just until they turn pink. Serve.

Nutrition: Calories: 487 Fat: 5 g Protein: 64 g Carbs: 26 g Fiber: 9 g Sugar: 3 g Sodium: 196 mg

Shrimp and Broccoli

Preparation time: 10 minutes

Cooking time: 5 minutes

Servings: 2

Ingredients:

> 1 tablespoon olive oil
> 1 clove of garlic, minced
> 1-pound shrimp
> 1/4 cup red bell pepper
> 1 cup broccoli florets, steamed
> 10-ounce cream cheese
> 1/2 teaspoon garlic powder
> 1/4 cup lemon juice
> 3/4 teaspoon ground peppercorns
> 1/4 cup half and half creamer

Directions:

1. Pour the oil and cook garlic for 30 seconds.
2. Add shrimp and cook for 2 minutes.
3. Add the rest of the ingredients.
4. Mix well. Cook for 2 minutes.

Nutrition: Calories: 469 Fat: 28 g Protein: 28 g
Carbs: 28 g Fiber: 2.6 g Sugars: 3.79 g Sodium: 374 mg

Tuna Carbonara

Preparation time: 5 minutes

Cooking time: 25 minutes

Servings: 2

Ingredients:

> 1/2 lb. tuna fillet, cut into pieces
> Two eggs
> 4 tbsp. fresh parsley, diced

What you'll need from the store cupboard:

> 1/2 Homemade Pasta, cook & drain,
> 1/2 cup reduced-fat parmesan cheese
> 2 cloves garlic, peeled
> 2 tbsp. extra virgin olive oil
> Salt & pepper to taste

Directions:

1. In a small bowl, beat the eggs, parmesan and a dash of pepper.
2. Heat the oil in a large skillet over med-high heat. Add garlic and cook until browned. Add the tuna and cook for 2-3 minutes, or until the tuna is almost cooked through. Discard the garlic.
3. Add the pasta and reduce the heat. Stir in egg mixture and cook, constantly stirring, for 2 minutes. If the sauce is too thick, thin with water, a little bit at a time until it has a creamy texture.
4. Salt and pepper to taste and serve garnished with parsley.

Nutrition: Calories: 409 Fat: 30 g Protein: 25 g
Carbs: 7 g Fiber: 1 g Sugar: 3 g Sodium: 97 mg

Tuna Patties

Preparation time: 5 minutes

Cooking time: 10 minutes

Servings: 4

Ingredients:

> 1 pound (454 g) canned tuna, drained
> 1 cup whole-wheat bread crumbs
> 2 large eggs, beaten
> ½ onion, grated
> 1 tablespoon chopped fresh dill
> Juice and zest of 1 lemon
> 3 tablespoons extra-virgin olive oil
> ½ cup tartar sauce for serving

Direction:

1. In a large bowl, combine the tuna, bread crumbs, eggs, onion, dill, lemon juice and zest. Form the mixture into 4 patties and chill for 10 minutes.
2. In a large nonstick skillet over medium-high heat, heat the olive oil until it shimmers. Add the patties and cook until browned on both sides, 4 to 5 minutes per side.
3. Serve topped with tartar sauce.

Nutrition: Calories: 530 Fat: 34 g Protein: 35 g Carbs: 18 g Sugars: 3 g Fiber: 2 g Sodium: 674 mg

Tomato Bun Tuna Melts

Preparation time: 5 minutes

Cooking time: 5 minutes

Servings: 2

Ingredients:

> 1 (5-ounce / 142-g) can chunk light tuna packed in water, drained
> 2 tablespoons plain nonfat Greek yogurt
> 2 teaspoons freshly squeezed lemon juice
> 2 tablespoons finely chopped celery
> 1 tablespoon finely chopped red onion
> Pinch cayenne pepper
> 1 large tomato, cut into ¾-inch-thick rounds
> ½ cup shredded Cheddar cheese

Direction:

1. Preheat the broiler to high.
2. In a medium bowl, combine the tuna, yogurt, lemon juice, celery, red onion, and cayenne pepper. Stir well.
3. Arrange the tomato slices on a baking sheet. Top each with some tuna salad and Cheddar cheese.
4. Broil for 3 to 4 minutes until the cheese is melted and bubbly. Serve.

Nutrition: Calories: 243 Fat: 10 g Protein: 30 g Carbs: 7 g Fiber: 1 g Sugars: 2 g Sodium: 444 mg

Snack And Appetizers

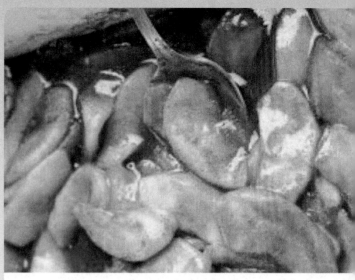

Baked Tuna with Asparagus

Preparation time: 10 minutes

Cooking time: 10 minutes

Servings: 2

Ingredients:

> 2 tuna steak
> 1 cup asparagus, trimmed
> 1 tsp. almond butter
> 1 tsp. rosemary
> 1/2 tsp. oregano
> 1/2 tsp. garlic powder
> 1tsp. lemon juice
> 1/2 tsp. ginger powder
> 1 tbsp. olive oil
> 1 tsp. red chili powder
> Salt and pepper to taste

Directions:

1. Marinate the tuna using oregano, lemon juice, salt, pepper, red chili powder, garlic, and ginger, and let it sit for 10 minutes.
2. In a pan, add the olive oil. Fry the tuna steaks for 2 minutes per side.
3. In another pan, melt the almond butter.
4. Toss the asparagus with salt, pepper, and rosemary for 3 minutes. Serve.

Nutrition: Calories: 351 Fat: 4.7 g Protein: 32 g Carbs: 3.2 g Fiber: 4.1 g Sugar: 12 g Sodium: 98.5 mg

Braised Apples

Preparation time: 5 minutes

Cooking time: 12 minutes

Servings: 2

Ingredients:

> 2 cored apples
> ½ cup of water
> ½ cup red wine
> 3 tbsp. sugar or stevia
> ½ tsp. ground cinnamon

Directions:

1. In the bottom of the Instant Pot, add the water and place apples.
2. Pour wine on top and sprinkle with sugar and cinnamon. Close the lid carefully and cook for 10 minutes at HIGH PRESSURE.
3. When done, do a quick pressure release.
4. Transfer the apples onto serving plates and top with cooking liquid.
5. Serve immediately.

Nutrition: Calories: 245 Fat: 0.5 g Carbs: 53 g Protein: 1 g Fiber: 2.6 g Sugar: 35 g Sodium: 153 mg

Cheesy Garlic Sweet Potatoes

Preparation time: 10 minutes

Cooking time: 25 minutes

Servings: 2

Ingredients:

> Sea salt to taste
> ¼ cup garlic butter melt
> ¾ cup shredded mozzarella cheese
> ½ cup of parmesan cheese freshly grated
> 4 medium-sized sweet potatoes
> 2 tsp freshly chopped parsley

Directions:

1. Heat the oven to 400 degrees Fahrenheit and brush the potatoes with garlic butter and season each with pepper and salt. Arrange the cut side down on a greased baking sheet until the flesh is tender or they turn golden brown.

2. Remove them from the oven, flip the cut side up and top up with parsley and parmesan cheese.

3. Change the settings of your instant fryer oven to broil and on medium heat, add the cheese and melt it. Sprinkle salt and pepper to taste. Serve them warm

Nutrition: Calories: 356 Fat: 9g Protein: 5g

Carbs: 13g Fiber: 4.1 g Sugar: 23 g Sodium: 345 mg

Chili Mango and Watermelon Salsa

Preparation time: 5 minutes

Cooking time: 0 minutes

Servings: 2

Ingredients:

> 1 red tomato, chopped
> Salt and black pepper to the taste
> 1 cup watermelon, seedless, peeled, and cubed
> 1 red onion, chopped
> 2 mangos, peeled and chopped
> 2 chili peppers, chopped
> ¼ cup cilantro, chopped
> 3 tablespoons lime juice
> Pita chips for serving

Directions:

1. In a bowl, mix the tomato with the watermelon, the onion and the rest of the ingredients except the pita chips and toss well.

2. Divide the mix into small cups and serve with pita chips on the side.

Nutrition: Calories: 62 Fat: 4g Protein: 2.3 g

Carbs: 3.9 g Fiber: 1.3 g Sugar: 32 g Sodium: 245 mg

Chocolate Fondue

Preparation time: 5 minutes

Cooking time: 10 minutes

Servings: 2

Ingredients:

> 1 cup water
> ½ tsp. sugar or stevia
> ½ cup coconut cream
> ¾ cup dark chocolate, chopped

Directions:

1. Pour the water into your Instant Pot.
2. To a heatproof bowl, add the chocolate, sugar, and coconut cream.
3. Place in the Instant Pot.
4. Seal the lid, select MANUAL, and cook for 2 minutes. When ready, do a quick release and carefully open the lid. Stir well and serve immediately.

Nutrition: Calories: 216 Fat: 17 g Protein: 2 g Carbs: 11 g Fiber: 2.4 g Sugar: 16 g Sodium: 633 mg

Creamy Spinach and Shallots Dip

Preparation time: 10 minutes

Cooking time: 0 minutes

Servings: 2

Ingredients:

> 1 pound spinach, roughly chopped
> 2 shallots, chopped
> 2 tablespoons mint, chopped
> ¾ cup cream cheese, soft
> Salt and black pepper to the taste

Directions:

1. In a blender, combine the spinach with the shallots and the rest of the ingredients, and pulse well.
2. Divide into small bowls and serve as a party dip.

Nutrition: Calories: 204 Fat: 11.5 g Protein: 5.9 g Carbs: 4.2 g Fiber: 3.1 g Sugar: 14 g Sodium: 241 mg

Cucumber Rolls

Preparation time: 5 minutes

Cooking time: 0 minutes

Servings: 2

Ingredients:

> 1 big cucumber, sliced lengthwise
> 1 tablespoon parsley, chopped
> 8 ounces canned tuna, drained and mashed
> Salt and black pepper to the taste
> 1 teaspoon lime juice

Directions:

1. Arrange cucumber slices on a working surface, divide the rest of the ingredients, and roll.
2. Arrange all the rolls on a platter and serve as an appetizer.

Nutrition: Calories: 200 Fat: 6 g Protein: 3.5 g Carbs: 7.6 g Fiber: 3.4 g Sugar: 12 g Sodium: 245 mg

Cucumber Sandwich Bites

Preparation time: 5 minutes

Cooking time: 0 minutes

Servings: 12

Ingredients:

> 1 cucumber, sliced
> 8 slices of whole-wheat bread
> 2 tablespoons cream cheese, soft
> 1 tablespoon chives, chopped
> ¼ cup avocado, peeled, pitted and mashed
> 1 teaspoon mustard
> Salt and black pepper to the taste

Directions:

1. Spread the mashed avocado on each bread slice, also spread the rest of the ingredients except the cucumber slices.
2. Divide the cucumber slices into the bread slices, cut each slice in thirds, arrange on a platter and serve as an appetizer.

Nutrition: Calories 187 Fat 12.4 g Protein 8.2 g Carbs 4.5 g Fiber 2.1 g Sugar: 14 g Sodium: 345 mg

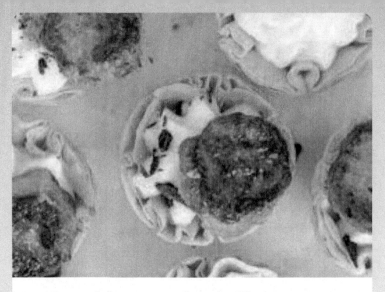

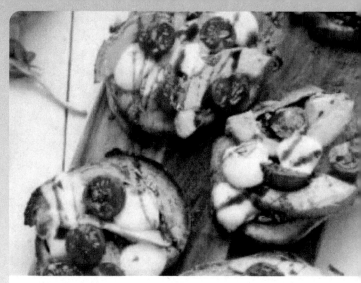

Glazed Bananas in Phyllo Nut Cups

Preparation time: 30 minutes

Cooking time: 45 minutes

Servings: 2

Ingredients:

> 3/4 cup shelled pistachios
> 1 teaspoon. ground cinnamon
> 4 sheets of phyllo dough (14 in x 9 in)
> 1/4 cup butter, melted

> **Sauce:**
> 3/4 cup butter, cubed
> 3 medium firm bananas, sliced
> 1/4 teaspoon. ground cinnamon
> 3 to 4 cups vanilla ice cream

Directions:

1. Finely chop pistachios in a food processor; move to a bowl, then mix in cinnamon. Slice each phyllo sheet into 6 four-inch squares, and get rid of the trimmings. Pile the squares, then use plastic wrap to cover.

2. Slather melted butter on each square one at a time, then scatter a heaping tablespoonful of pistachio mixture. Pile 3 squares, and flip each at an angle to misalign the corners. Force each stack on the sides and bottom of an oiled eight-oz. Custard cup. Bake for 15-20 minutes in a 350 degrees F oven until golden; cool for 5 minutes. Move to a wire rack to cool completely.

3. Melt and boil butter in a saucepan to make the sauce; lower the heat. Mix in cinnamon and bananas gently; heat completely. Put ice cream in the phyllo cups until full, then put banana sauce on top. Serve right away.

Nutrition: Calories: 735 Fat: 45 g Protein: 7 g
Carbs: 82 g Fiber: 3 g Sugar: 25 g Sodium: 468 mg

Grilled Avocado Caprese Crostini

Preparation time: 10 minutes

Cooking time: 20 minutes

Servings: 2

Ingredients:

> 1 avocado thinly sliced
> 9 ounces ripened cherry tomatoes
> ounces fresh bocconcini in water
> 2 tsp balsamic glaze
> 8 pieces of Italian baguette
> ½ a cup basil leaves

Directions:

1. Preheat your oven to 375 degrees Fahrenheit

2. Arrange your baking sheet properly before spraying them on top with olive oil.

3. Bake your item of choice until they are well done or golden brown. Rub your crostini with the cut side of garlic while they are still warm and you can season them with pepper and salt.

4. Divide the basil leaves on each side of the bread and top up with tomato halves, avocado slices and bocconcini. Season it with pepper and salt.

5. Broil it for 4 minutes and when the cheese starts to melt through, remove and drizzle balsamic glaze before serving.

Nutrition: Calories: 278 Fat: 10 g Protein: 10 g
Carbs: 37 g Fiber: 2.54 g Sugar: 21 g Sodium: 342 mg

Instant Popcorn

Preparation time: 1 minute

Cooking time: 5 minutes

Servings: 2

Ingredients:

> 2 tablespoons coconut oil
> ½ cup popcorn kernels
> ¼ cup margarine spread, melted, optional
> Sea salt to taste

Direction:

1. Set the Instant Pot to Sauté. Melt the coconut oil in the inner pot, then add the popcorn kernels and stir.
2. Press Adjust to bring the temperature up to high. When the corn starts popping, secure the lid on the Instant Pot.
3. When you no longer hear popping, turn off the Instant Pot, remove the lid, and pour the popcorn into a bowl. Top with the optional melted margarine and season the popcorn with sea salt to your liking.

Nutrition: Calories: 161 Fat: 12 g Protein: 1 g Carbs: 13 g Fiber: 3 g Sugars: 0 g Sodium: 89 mg

Healthy Cookies

Preparation time: 4 minutes

Cooking time: 15 minutes

Servings: 2

Ingredients:

> 1 ¾ cup of quick oats
> 2 large ripe bananas
> 4 tsp peanut butter
> 1/3 cup crushed nuts of your choice
> ½ tsp pure vanilla extract
> ¼ cup shredded coconut

Directions:

1. Preheat your oven to 350 degrees Fahrenheit.
2. Mash the bananas in a bowl and add the oats and mix them well to combine. Fold any optional add-ins, such as ¼ cup chocolate chips. You can add honey to the taste.
3. Line your baking tray with parchment paper and drop one tsp of cookie dough per cookie into your tray. Press down with a metal spoon into the shape of the cookies.
4. Bake for 20 minutes depending on your oven, or cook them until they are golden brown on top.
5. Remove and allow to cool before serving.

Nutrition: Calories: 24 Fat: 46 g Proteins: 1 g Carbs: 5 g Fiber: 2.67 g Sugar: 12 g Sodium: 522 mg

Hummus with Ground Lamb

Preparation Time: 10 minutes

Cooking Time: 15 minutes

Servings: 8

Ingredients:

> 10 ounces hummus

> 12 ounces lamb meat, ground

> ½ cup pomegranate seeds

> ¼ cup parsley, chopped

> 1 tablespoon olive oil

> Pita chips for serving

Directions:

1. Heat up a pan with the oil over medium-high heat, add the meat, and brown for 15 minutes, stirring often.

2. Spread the hummus on a platter, spread the ground lamb all over, also spread the pomegranate seeds and the parsley, and serve with pita chips as a snack.

Nutrition: Calories 133 Fat 9.7 g Protein 5 g

Carbs 6.4 g Fiber 1.7 g Sugar: 24 g Sodium: 352 mg

Lemon Artichokes

Preparation time: 5 minutes

Cooking time: 5 to 15 minutes

Servings: 2

Ingredients:

> 4 artichokes

> 1 cup water

> 2 tablespoons lemon juice

> 1 teaspoon salt

Direction:

1. Wash and trim artichokes by cutting off the stems flush with the bottoms of the artichokes and by cutting ¾–1 inch off the tops. Stand upright in the bottom of the inner pot of the Instant Pot.

2. Pour water, lemon juice, and salt over artichokes.

3. Secure the lid and make sure the vent is set to sealing. On Manual, set the Instant Pot for 15 minutes for large artichokes, 10 minutes for medium artichokes, or 5 minutes for small artichokes.

4. When cook time is up, perform a quick release by releasing the pressure manually.

Nutrition: Calories: 60 Fat: 0 g Protein: 4 g

Carbs: 13 g Fiber: 6 g Sugars: 1 g Sodium: 397 mg

Pan-Fried Trout

Preparation time: 15 minutes

Cooking time: 10 minutes

Servings: 2

Ingredients:

> 1 ¼ pounds trout fillets
> 1/3 cup white or yellow cornmeal
> ¼ teaspoon anise seeds
> ¼ teaspoon black pepper
> ½ cup minced cilantro, or parsley
> Vegetable cooking spray
> Lemon wedges

Directions:

1. Coat fish with combined cornmeal, spices, and cilantro, pressing it gently into the fish. Spray large skillet with cooking spray; heat over medium heat until hot.
2. Add fish and cook until fish is tender and flakes with a fork, about 5 minutes on each side. Serve with lemon wedges.

Nutrition: Calories: 207 Fat: 16 g Protein: 18g
Carbs: 19 g Fiber: 4 g Sugar: 22 g Sodium: 486

Personal Pizza Biscuit

Preparation time: 5 minutes

Cooking time: 15 minutes

Servings: 2

Ingredients:

> 1 sachet select
> Buttermilk Cheddar Herb Biscuit.
> 2 tbsp. cold water
> Cooking spray
> 2 tbsp. no-sugar-added tomato sauce
> 1/4 cup reduced-fat shredded cheese

Directions:

1. Preheat the oven to 350°F.
2. Mix biscuit and water, and spread mixture into a small, circular crust shape onto a greased, foil-lined baking sheet.
3. Bake for 10 minutes.
4. Top with tomato sauce and cheese, and cook till cheese is melted, about 5 minutes.

Nutrition: Calories 345 Fats: 3.2 g Protein: 3.6 g
Carbs: 125 g Fiber: 2.7 g Sugar: 15 g Sodium: 10.5 mg

Raspberry Compote

Preparation time: 11 minutes

Cooking time: 30 minutes

Servings: 2

Ingredients:

> 1 cup raspberries
> ½ cup Swerve
> 1 tsp freshly grated lemon zest
> 1 tsp vanilla extract
> 2 cups water

Directions:

1. Press the SAUTÉ button on your Instant Pot, then add all the listed ingredients.
2. Stir well and pour in 1 cup of water. Cook for 5 minutes, continually stirring, then pour in 1 more cup of water and press the CANCEL button.
3. Secure the lid properly, press the MANUAL button, and set the timer to 15 minutes on LOW pressure. When the timer buzzes, press the CANCEL button and release the pressure naturally for 10minutes.
4. Move the pressure handle to the "venting" position to release any remaining pressure and open the lid. Let it cool before serving.

Nutrition: Calories: 48 Fat: 0.5 g Protein: 1 g Carbs: 5 g Fiber: 2.6 g Sugar: 34 g Sodium: 232 mg

Salmon Apple Salad Sandwich

Preparation time: 15 minutes

Cooking time: 10 minutes

Servings: 2

Ingredients:

> 4 ounces (125 g) canned pink salmon, drained and flaked
> 1 medium (180 g) red apple, cored and diced
> 1 celery stalk (about 60 g), chopped
> 1 shallot (about 40 g), finely chopped
> 1/3 cup (85 g) light mayonnaise
> 8 slices of whole-grain bread (about 30 g each), toasted
> 8 (15 g) Romaine lettuce leaves
> Salt and freshly ground black pepper

Directions:

1. Combine the salmon, apple, celery, shallot, and mayonnaise in a mixing bowl. Season with salt and pepper.
2. Place 1 slice of bread on a plate, top with lettuce and salmon salad, and then covers with another slice of bread. Repeat the procedure for the remaining ingredients.
3. Serve and enjoy.

Nutrition: Calories: 315 Fat 11.3 g Protein 15.1 g Carbs 40.4 g Fiber: 3.12 g Sugar: 24 g Sodium 469 mg

Salmon Cream Cheese and Onion on Bagel

Preparation time: 15 minutes

Cooking time: 10 minutes

Servings: 2

Ingredients:

> 8 ounces (250 g) smoked salmon fillet, thinly sliced
> 1/2 cup (125 g) cream cheese
> 1 medium (110 g) onion, thinly sliced
> 4 bagels (about 80g each), split
> 2 tablespoons (7 g) fresh parsley, chopped
> Freshly ground black pepper, to taste

Directions:

1. Spread the cream cheese on each bottom half of the bagels. Top with salmon and onion, season with pepper, sprinkle with parsley and then cover with bagel tops.
2. Serve and enjoy.

Nutrition: Calories: 309 Fat 14.1 g Protein 14.7 g Carbs 32.0 g Fiber: 3.1 g Sugar: 16 g Sodium 571 mg

Salmon Feta and Pesto Wrap

Preparation time: 15 minutes

Cooking time: 10 minutes

Servings: 2

Ingredients:

> 8 ounces (250 g) smoked salmon fillet, thinly sliced
> 1 cup (150 g) feta cheese
> 8 (15 g) Romaine lettuce leaves
> 4 (6-inch) pita bread
> 1/4 cup (60 g) basil pesto sauce

Directions:

1. Place 1 pita bread on a plate. Top with lettuce, salmon, feta cheese, and pesto sauce. Fold or roll to enclose filling. Repeat the procedure for the remaining ingredients.
2. Serve and enjoy.

Nutrition: Calories: 379 Fat 17.7 g Protein: 18.4 g Carbs: 36.6 g Fiber: 1.3 g Sugar: 21 g Sodium: 554 mg

Smoked Salmon and Cheese on Rye Bread

Preparation time: 15 minutes

Cooking time: 10 minutes

Servings: 2

Ingredients:

> 8 ounces (250 g) smoked salmon, thinly sliced
> 1/3 cup (85 g) mayonnaise
> 2 tablespoons (30 ml) lemon juice
> 1 tablespoon (15 g) Dijon mustard
> 1 teaspoon (3 g) garlic, minced
> 4 slices of cheddar cheese (about 2 oz. or 30 g each)
> 8 slices of rye bread (about 2 oz. or 30 g each)
> 8 (15 g) Romaine lettuce leaves
> Salt and freshly ground black pepper

Directions:

1. Mix together the mayonnaise, lemon juice, mustard, and garlic in a small bowl. Flavor with salt and pepper and set aside.
2. Spread dressing on 4 bread slices. Top with lettuce, salmon, and cheese. Cover with remaining rye bread slices.
3. Serve and enjoy.

Nutrition: Calories: 365 Fat: 16.6 g Protein: 18.8 g Carbs: 31.6 g Fiber: 3.5 g Sugar: 32 g Sodium: 951 mg

Wrapped Plums

Preparation time: 5 minutes

Cooking time: 0 minutes

Servings: 8

Ingredients:

> 2 ounces prosciutto, cut into 16 pieces
> 4 plums, quartered
> 1 tablespoon chives, chopped
> A pinch of red pepper flakes, crushed

Directions:

1. Wrap each plum quarter in a prosciutto slice, arrange them all on a platter, sprinkle the chives, and pepper flakes all over, and serve.

Nutrition: Calories: 30 Fat: 1 g Protein: 2 g Carbs: 4 g Fiber: 0 g

Soup And Stew

– RECIPES –

Awesome Chicken Enchilada Soup

Preparation time: 10 minutes

Cooking time: 30 minutes

Servings: 2

Ingredients:

- 2 tbsp coconut oil
- 1 lb. boneless, skinless chicken thighs
- ¾ cup red enchilada sauce, sugar-free
- ¼ cup water
- ¼ cup onion, chopped
- 3 oz canned diced green chilis
- 1 avocado, sliced
- 1 cup cheddar cheese, shredded
- ¼ cup pickled jalapeños, chopped
- ½ cup sour cream
- 1 tomato, diced

Directions:

1. Put a large pan over medium heat. Add coconut oil and warm. Place in the chicken and cook until browned on the outside. Stir in onion, chili, water, and enchilada sauce, then close with a lid.
2. Allow simmering for 20 minutes until the chicken is cooked through.
3. Spoon the soup in a serving bowl and top with the sauce, cheese, sour cream, tomato, and avocado.

Nutrition: Calories: 643 Fat: 44.2 g Protein: 45.8 g Carbs: 9.7 g Fiber: 2.5 g Sugar: 25 g Sodium: 261 mg

Beansprout Soup

Preparation time: 10 minutes

Cooking time: 30 minutes

Servings: 2

Ingredients:

- 1 lb. beansprouts
- 1 lb. chopped vegetables
- 1 cup low sodium broth
- 1 tbsp. mixed herbs
- 1 minced onion

Directions:

1. Mix all the ingredients in your Instant Pot, and cook on Stew for 10 minutes.
2. Release the pressure naturally and serve.

Nutrition: Calories: 100 Fat: 10 g Protein: 4g Carbs: 4 g Fiber: 5.5 g Sugar: 29 g Sodium: 310 mg

Broccoli Stilton Soup

Preparation time: 15 minutes

Cooking time: 35 minutes

Servings: 2

Ingredients:

> 1 lb. chopped broccoli
> 0.5 lb. chopped vegetables
> 1 cup low sodium vegetable broth
> 1 cup Stilton

Directions:

1. Mix all the ingredients in your Instant Pot.
2. Cook on Stew for 35 minutes.
3. Release the pressure naturally.
4. Blend the soup.

Nutrition: Calories: 280 Fat: 22 g Protein: 13 g Carbs: 9 g Fiber: 2.5 g Sugar: 2 g Sodium: 257 mg

Cheese Cream Soup with Chicken & Cilantro

Preparation time: 10 minutes

Cooking time: 30 minutes

Servings: 2

Ingredients:

> 1 carrot, chopped
> 1 onion, chopped
> 2 cups cooked and shredded chicken
> 3 tbsp butter
> 4 cups chicken broth
> 2 tbsp cilantro, chopped
> 1/3 cup buffalo sauce
> ½ cup cream cheese
> Salt and black pepper to taste

Directions:

1. In a skillet over medium heat, warm butter and sauté carrot and onion until tender, about 5 minutes.
2. Add to a food processor and blend with buffalo sauce and cream cheese until smooth. Transfer to a pot, add chicken broth and heat until hot but do not bring to a boil. Stir in chicken, salt, and pepper and cook until heated through. When ready, remove to soup bowls and serve garnished with cilantro.

Nutrition: Calories: 487 Fat: 41 g Protein: 16.3 g Carbs: 7.2 g Fiber: 2.5 g Sugar: 25 g Sodium: 251 mg

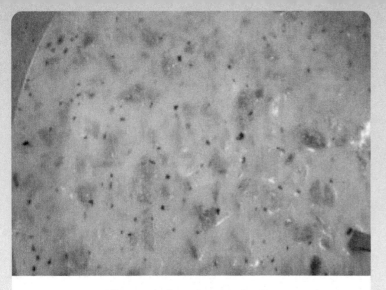

Cheeseburger Soup

Preparation time: 5 minutes

Cooking time: 25 minutes

Servings: 2

Ingredients:

> Avocado oil cooking spray
> ½ cup diced white onion
> ½ cup diced celery
> ½ cup sliced portobello mushrooms
> 1 pound (454 g) 93% lean ground beef
> 1 (15-ounce / 425-g) can no-salt-added diced tomatoes
> 2 cups low-sodium beef broth
> 1/3 cup half-and-half
> ¾ cup shredded sharp Cheddar cheese

Direction:

1. Heat a large stockpot over medium-low heat. When hot, coat the cooking surface with cooking spray. Put the onion, celery, and mushrooms into the pot. Cook for 7 minutes, stirring occasionally.
2. Add the ground beef and cook for 5 minutes, stirring and breaking apart as needed.
3. Add the diced tomatoes with their juices and the broth. Increase the heat to medium-high and simmer for 10 minutes. Remove the pot from the heat and stir in half-and-half.
4. Serve topped with the cheese.

Nutrition: Calories: 330 Fat: 18 g Protein: 33 g Carbs: 9 g Fiber: 2 g Sugars: 5 g Sodium: 321 mg

Chicken Zoodle Soup

Preparation time: 10 minutes

Cooking time: 30 minutes

Servings: 2

Ingredients:

> 1 lb. chopped cooked chicken
> 1 lb. spiralized zucchini
> 1 cup low sodium chicken soup
> 1 cup diced vegetables

Directions:

1. Mix all the ingredients except the zucchini in your Instant Pot.
2. Cook on Stew for 35 minutes.
3. Release the pressure naturally.
4. Stir in the zucchini and allow to heat thoroughly.

Nutrition: Calories: 250 Fat: 10 g Protein: 40 g Carbs: 5 g Fiber: 6.3 g Sugar: 0 g Sodium: 256 mg

French Onion Soup

Preparation time: 10 minutes

Cooking time: 30 minutes

Servings: 2

Ingredients:

> 6 onions, chopped finely
> 2 cups vegetable broth
> 2 tbsp. oil
> 2 tbsp. Gruyere

Directions:

1. Place the oil in your Instant Pot and cook the onions on Sauté until soft and brown.
2. Mix all the ingredients in your Instant Pot.
3. Cook on Stew for 35 minutes.
4. Release the pressure naturally.

Nutrition: Calories: 110 Fat: 10 g Protein: 3 g Carbs: 8 g Fiber: 3.6 g Sugar: 3 g Sodium: 254 mg

Irish Stew

Preparation time: 15 minutes

Cooking time: 35 minutes

Servings: 2

Ingredients:

> 1.5 lb. diced lamb shoulder
> 1 lb. chopped vegetables
> 1 cup low sodium beef broth
> 3 minced onions
> 1 tbsp. ghee

Directions:

1. Mix all the ingredients in your Instant Pot.
2. Cook on Stew for 35 minutes.
3. Release the pressure naturally.

Nutrition: Calories: 330 Fat: 12 g Protein: 49 g Carbs: 9 g Fiber: 7.1 g Sugar: 2 g Sodium: 257 mg

Kebab Stew

Preparation time: 15 minutes

Cooking time: 35 minutes

Servings: 2

Ingredients:

> 1 lb. cubed, seasoned kebab meat
> 1 lb. cooked chickpeas
> 1 cup low sodium vegetable broth
> 1 tbsp. black pepper

Directions:

1. Mix all the ingredients in your Instant Pot.
2. Cook on Stew for 35 minutes.
3. Release the pressure naturally.

Nutrition: Calories: 290 Fat: 10 g Protein: 34 g Carbs: 22 g Fiber: 1.5 g Sugar: 4 g Sodium: 415 mg

Lamb Stew

Preparation time: 15 minutes

Cooking time: 35 minutes

Servings: 2

Ingredients:

> 1 lb. diced lamb shoulder
> 1 lb. chopped winter vegetables
> 1 cup low sodium vegetable broth
> 1 tbsp. yeast extract
> 1 tbsp. star anise spice mix

Directions:

1. Mix all the ingredients in your Instant Pot.
2. Cook on Stew for 35 minutes.
3. Release the pressure naturally.

Nutrition: Calories: 320 Fat: 8 g Protein: 42 g Carbs: 10 g Fiber: 2.1 g Sugar: 2 g Sodium: 257 mg

Lentil Vegetable Soup

Preparation time: 10 minutes

Cooking time: 15 minutes

Servings: 2

Ingredients:

> 2 tablespoons extra-virgin olive oil
> 1 onion, finely chopped
> 1 carrot, chopped
> 1 cup chopped kale (stems removed)
> 3 garlic cloves, minced
> 1 cup canned lentils, drained and rinsed
> 5 cups unsalted vegetable broth
> 2 teaspoons dried rosemary (or 1 tablespoon chopped fresh rosemary)
> ½ teaspoon sea salt
> ¼ teaspoon freshly ground black pepper

Direction:

1. In a large pot over medium-high heat, heat the olive oil until it shimmers. Add the onion and carrot and cook, stirring, until the vegetables begin to soften, about 3 minutes. Add the kale and cook for 3 minutes more. Add the garlic and cook, constantly stirring, for 30 seconds.
2. Stir in the lentils, vegetable broth, rosemary, salt, and pepper. Bring to a simmer. Simmer, occasionally stirring, for 5 minutes more.

Nutrition: Calories: 160 Fat: 7 g Protein: 6 g Carbs: 19 g Fiber: 6 g Sugars: 12 g Sodium: 187 mg

Meatball Stew

Preparation time: 15 minutes

Cooking time: 25 minutes

Servings: 2

Ingredients:

> 1 lb. sausage meat
> 2 cups chopped tomato
> 1 cup chopped vegetables
> 2 tbsp. Italian seasonings
> 1 tbsp. vegetable oil

Directions:

1. Roll the sausage into meatballs.
2. Put the Instant Pot on Sauté and fry the meatballs in the oil until brown.
3. Mix all the ingredients in your Instant Pot.
4. Cook on Stew for 25 minutes.
5. Release the pressure naturally.

Nutrition: Calories: 300 Fat: 12 g Protein: 40 g Carbs: 4 g Fiber: 1.3 g Sugar: 1 g Sodium: 567 mg

Meatless Ball Soup

Preparation time: 15 minutes

Cooking time: 15 minutes

Servings: 2

Ingredients:

> 1 lb. minced tofu
> 0.5 lb. chopped vegetables
> 2 cups low sodium vegetable broth
> 1 tbsp. almond flour
> salt and pepper to taste

Directions:

1. Mix the tofu, flour, salt and pepper.
2. Form the meatballs.
3. Place all the ingredients in your Instant Pot.
4. Cook on Stew for 15 minutes.
5. Release the pressure naturally.

Nutrition: Calories: 240 Fat: 10 g Protein: 35 g Carbs: 9 g Fiber: 1.4 g Sugar: 3 g Sodium: 423 mg

Quick Clam Chowder

Preparation time: 10 minutes

Cooking time: 15 minutes

Servings: 2

Ingredients:

> 2 tablespoons extra-virgin olive oil
> 3 slices of pepper bacon, chopped
> 1 onion, chopped
> 1 red bell pepper, seeded and chopped
> 1 fennel bulb, chopped
> 3 tablespoons flour
> 5 cups low-sodium or unsalted chicken broth
> 6 ounces (170 g) chopped canned clams, undrained
> ½ teaspoon sea salt
> ½ cup milk

Direction:

1. In a large pot over medium-high heat, heat the olive oil until it shimmers. Add the bacon and cook, stirring, until browned, about 4 minutes. Remove the bacon from the fat with a slotted spoon, and set it aside on a plate.
2. Add the onion, bell pepper, and fennel to the fat in the pot. Cook, occasionally stirring, until the vegetables are soft, about 5 minutes. Add the flour and cook, constantly stirring, for 1 minute. Add the broth, clams, and salt. Bring to a simmer. Cook, stirring, until the soup thickens, about 5 minutes more.
3. Stir in the milk and return the bacon to the pot. Cook, stirring, 1 minute more.

Nutrition: Calories: 335 Fat: 20 g Protein: 20 g Carbs: 21 g Fiber: 3 g Sugars: 6 g Sodium: 496 mg

30-Days Meal Plan

Day	Breakfast	Snacks	Lunch	Snacks	Dinner
1	Apple Topped French Toast	Baked Potato Topped with Cream cheese 'n Olives	Asian Chicken Stir-Fry	Glazed Bananas in Phyllo Nut Cups	Grilled Lime Chicken
2	Breakfast Sandwich	Bell Pepper-Corn Wrapped in Tortilla	Bacon and Chicken Garlic Wrap	Instant Popcorn	Grilled Tuna Steaks
3	Buckwheat Porridge	Black Bean Burger with Garlic-Chipotle	Baked Salmon with Garlic Parmesan Topping	Lemon Artichokes	Ground Chicken Meatballs
4	Hawaiian Breakfast Bake	Brussels Sprouts with Balsamic Oil	Baked Turkey Spaghetti	Pan-Fried Trout	Honey Mustard Roasted Salmon
5	Jicama Hash Browns	Chicken, Cantaloupe, Kale, and Almond Salad	Beef and Zucchini Meatballs	Salmon Apple Salad Sandwich	Lamb Burgers with Mushrooms and Cheese
6	Pumpkin Spice French Toast	Creamy Cauliflower and Broccoli	Beef Burrito Bowl	Salmon Cream Cheese and Onion on Bagel	Lamb Kofta Meatballs with Cucumber Salad

7	Salty Macadamia Chocolate Smoothie	Cucumber Tomato Avocado Salad	Beef Korma Curry	Salmon Feta and Pesto Wrap	Lemon and Honey Pork Tenderloin
8	Savory Keto Pancake	Simple Green Beans with Butter	Blackened Chicken Bake	Smoked Salmon and Cheese on Rye Bread	Lemon Greek Beef and Vegetables
9	Steel-Cut Oatmeal Bowl with Fruit and Nuts	Sofrito Steak Salad	Cajun Catfish	Healthy Cookies	Lemon Pepper Salmon
10	Strawberry Kiwi Smoothies	Tomato, Peach, and Strawberry Salad	Cajun Shrimp and Roasted Vegetables	Grilled Avocado Caprese Crostini	Low-Fat Steak
11	Sweet Potato Waffles	Young Kale and Cabbage Salad	Chicken Caesar Salad	Cheesy Garlic Sweet Potatoes	Meatloaf Reboot
12	Tropical Yogurt Kiwi Bowl	Cucumber-Carrot Salad	Chicken in Wine	Personal Pizza Biscuit	Mustard Glazed Pork Chops
13	Egg Salad Sandwiches	Fruity Tuna Salad	Chicken Romaine Salad	Cucumber Rolls	One-Pan Chicken Dinner
14	Cinnamon Apple Oatmeal	Lemon-Basil Strawberry Salad	Chicken Romaine Salad	Chili Mango and Watermelon Salsa	Open-Faced Tuna Melts
15	Egg White Zucchini Frittata	Tart Cabbage Side Salad	Chipotle Chili Pork Chops	Creamy Spinach and Shallots Dip	Orange Chicken
16	Mushroom and Spinach Scrambled Eggs	Cheesy Mushroom and Pesto Flatbreads	Cilantro Lime Grilled Shrimp	Hummus with Ground Lamb	Oregano Chicken Breast
17	Oatmeal Yogurt Breakfast	Honey Roasted Carrots	Cioppino	Cucumber Sandwich Bites	Parmesan-Crusted Pork Chops
18	Pumpkin Walnut Oatmeal	Grilled Portobello and Zucchini Burger	Cod with Mango Salsa	Wrapped Plums	Peppered Beef with Greens and Beans
19	Raisin French Toast	Bell Pepper Black Olive Salad	Country-Style Pork Ribs	Baked Tuna with Asparagus	Peppered Chicken with Balsamic Kale

20	Fish With Fresh Herb Sauce	Chestnut Lettuce Wraps	Couscous and Sweet Potatoes with Pork	Yogurt Mint	Pork Chops with Raspberry-Chipotle Sauce and Herbed Rice
21	Salad With Ranch	Kale and Carrot Veggie Soup	Crab Frittata	Chocolate Fondue	Pork Medallions with Cherry Sauce
22	Apple Topped French Toast	Egg Pea Mix wrapped in Kale Leaves	Creamy Asparagus Veggie Soup Bowl	Raspberry Compote	Pork on a Blanket
23	Breakfast Sandwich	Baked Potato Topped with Cream cheese 'n Olives	Crunchy Lemon Shrimp	Braised Apples	Quick & Juicy Pork Chops
24	Buckwheat Porridge	Bell Pepper-Corn Wrapped in Tortilla	Curried Pork and Vegetable Skewers	Glazed Bananas in Phyllo Nut Cups	Red Clam Sauce and Pasta
25	Hawaiian Breakfast Bake	Black Bean Burger with Garlic-Chipotle	Curried Tuna Salad Lettuce Wraps	Instant Popcorn	Roll-Ups from Mexico
26	Jicama Hash Browns	Brussels Sprouts with Balsamic Oil	Diet Boiled Ribs	Lemon Artichokes	Rosemary Lamb Chops
27	Pumpkin Spice French Toast	Chicken, Cantaloupe, Kale, and Almond Salad	Easy Salmon Stew	Pan-Fried Trout	Saffron Chicken
28	Salty Macadamia Chocolate Smoothie	Creamy Cauliflower and Broccoli	Fish with Mushrooms	Salmon Apple Salad Sandwich	Salmon Milano
29	Savory Keto Pancake	Cucumber Tomato Avocado Salad	Fried Pork Chops	Salmon Cream Cheese and Onion on Bagel	Savory Rubbed Roast Chicken
30	Steel-Cut Oatmeal Bowl with Fruit and Nuts	Simple Green Beans with Butter	Greek Chicken	Salmon Feta and Pesto Wrap	Fish with Mushrooms

Appendix 1: Measurements Conversion Chart

Appendix 2: Recipes Index

delish

UK/US CONVERSION CHART

DRY INGREDIENTS

INGREDIENT	GRAMS	CUPS
All-Purpose Flour	120 grams	1 cup
Baking Powder	4 grams	1 tsp
Baking Soda	3 grams	½ tsp
Brown Sugar (packed)	213 grams	1 cup
Confectioners' Sugar	113 grams	1 cup
Cornmeal (ground)	156 grams	1 cup
Cornstarch	28 grams	¼ cup
Chocolate Chips	170 grams	1 cup
Cocoa Powder (unsweetened)	42 grams	½ cup
Granulated Sugar	198 grams	1 cup
Whole Wheat Flour	113 grams	1 cup

WET INGREDIENTS

INGREDIENT	GRAMS	CUPS
Butter	113 grams	½ cup
Buttermilk	227 grams	1 cup
Corn Syrup	312 grams	1 cup
Heavy Cream	227 grams	1 cup
Eggs	50 grams	1 large
Milk	227 grams	1 cup
Vegetable Oil	198 grams	1 cup
Vegetable Shortening	46 grams	¼ cup
Vanilla Extract	14 grams	1 tbsp

TEMPERATURES

CELSIUS	150°	165°	177°	190°	200°	220°	230°	245°	260°
FAHRENHEIT	300°	325°	350°	375°	400°	425°	450°	475°	500°

Breakfast

Apple Topped French Toast
Breakfast Sandwich
Buckwheat Porridge
Cinnamon Apple Oatmeal
Egg Salad Sandwiches
Egg White Zucchini Frittata
Fish With Fresh Herb Sauce
Hawaiian Breakfast Bake
Jicama Hash Browns
Mushroom and Spinach Scrambled Eggs
Oatmeal Yogurt Breakfast
Pumpkin Spice French Toast
Pumpkin Walnut Oatmeal
Raisin French Toast
Salad With Ranch
Salty Macadamia Chocolate Smoothie
Savory Keto Pancake
Steel-Cut Oatmeal Bowl with Fruit and Nuts
Strawberry Kiwi Smoothies
Sweet Potato Waffles
Tropical Yogurt Kiwi Bowl

Vegetables and Salads

Baked Potato Topped with Cream cheese 'n Olives
Bell Pepper Black Olive Salad
Bell Pepper-Corn Wrapped in Tortilla
Black Bean Burger with Garlic-Chipotle
Brussels Sprouts with Balsamic Oil

Cheesy Mushroom and Pesto Flatbreads
Chestnut Lettuce Wraps
Chicken, Cantaloupe, Kale, and Almond Salad
Creamy Cauliflower and Broccoli
Cucumber Tomato Avocado Salad
Cucumber-Carrot Salad
Egg Pea Mix wrapped in Kale Leaves
Fruity Tuna Salad
Grilled Portobello and Zucchini Burger
Honey Roasted Carrots
Kale and Carrot Veggie Soup
Lemon-Basil Strawberry Salad
Simple Green Beans with Butter
Sofrito Steak Salad
Tart Cabbage Side Salad
Tomato, Peach, and Strawberry Salad
Young Kale and Cabbage Salad

Beef, Pork and Lamb

Beef and Zucchini Meatballs
Beef Burrito Bowl
Beef Korma Curry
Chipotle Chili Pork Chops
Country-Style Pork Ribs
Couscous and Sweet Potatoes with Pork
Creamy Asparagus Veggie Soup Bowl
Curried Pork and Vegetable Skewers
Diet Boiled Ribs
Fried Pork Chops
Lamb Burgers with Mushrooms and Cheese
Lamb Kofta Meatballs with Cucumber Salad
Lemon and Honey Pork Tenderloin
Lemon Greek Beef and Vegetables
Low-Fat Steak
Meatloaf Reboot
Mustard Glazed Pork Chops
Parmesan-Crusted Pork Chops

Peppered Beef with Greens and Beans
Pork Chops with Raspberry-Chipotle Sauce and Herbed Rice
Pork Medallions with Cherry Sauce
Pork on a Blanket
Quick & Juicy Pork Chops
Roll-Ups from Mexico
Rosemary Lamb Chops
Za'atar Lamb Chops

Poultry

Asian Chicken Stir-Fry
Bacon and Chicken Garlic Wrap
Baked Turkey Spaghetti
Blackened Chicken Bake
Chicken Caesar Salad
Chicken in Wine
Chicken Romaine Salad
Greek Chicken
Grilled Lime Chicken
Ground Chicken Meatballs
One-Pan Chicken Dinner
Orange Chicken
Oregano Chicken Breast
Peppered Chicken with Balsamic Kale
Saffron Chicken
Savory Rubbed Roast Chicken
Smothered Dijon Chicken
Teriyaki Meatballs
Turkey Chili
Turkey Meatballs
Turkey Meatloaf Muffins

Fish and Seafood

Baked Salmon with Garlic Parmesan Topping
Cajun Catfish
Cajun Shrimp and Roasted Vegetables

Cilantro Lime Grilled Shrimp
Cioppino
Cod with Mango Salsa
Crab Frittata
Crunchy Lemon Shrimp
Curried Tuna Salad Lettuce Wraps
Easy Salmon Stew
Fish with Mushrooms
Grilled Tuna Steaks
Honey Mustard Roasted Salmon
Lemon Pepper Salmon
Open-Faced Tuna Melts
Red Clam Sauce and Pasta
Salmon Milano
Shrimp and Artichoke Skillet
Shrimp and Broccoli
Tomato Bun Tuna Melts
Tuna Carbonara
Tuna Patties
Whole Veggie-Stuffed Trout

Snack and Appetizers

Baked Tuna with Asparagus
Braised Apples
Cheesy Garlic Sweet Potatoes
Chili Mango and Watermelon Salsa
Chocolate Fondue
Creamy Spinach and Shallots Dip
Cucumber Rolls
Cucumber Sandwich Bites
Glazed Bananas in Phyllo Nut Cups
Grilled Avocado Caprese Crostini
Healthy Cookies
Hummus with Ground Lamb
Instant Popcorn
Lemon Artichokes

Pan-Fried Trout
Personal Pizza Biscuit
Raspberry Compote
Salmon Apple Salad Sandwich
Salmon Cream Cheese and Onion on Bagel
Salmon Feta and Pesto Wrap
Smoked Salmon and Cheese on Rye Bread
Wrapped Plums
Yogurt Mint

Soup and Stew

Awesome Chicken Enchilada Soup
Beansprout Soup
Broccoli Stilton Soup
Cheese Cream Soup with Chicken & Cilantro
Cheeseburger Soup
Chicken Zoodle Soup
French Onion Soup
Irish Stew
Kebab Stew
Lamb Stew
Lentil Vegetable Soup
Meatball Stew
Meatless Ball Soup
Pumpkin Soup
Quick Clam Chowder
Shiitake Soup
Spicy Pepper Soup
Sweet and Sour Soup
Taco Soup
Tuscan Beef Stew
Zucchini Soup
Zucchini-Basil Soup

Conclusion

Type 2 Diabetes Cookbook is a great cookbook with recipes for people who have their own Type 2 diabetes. The book has everything you need for your diabetic diet, including information about the food's type of carbohydrates and how healthy it is if you have type 2 diabetes. It also includes breakfast, lunch, and dinner ideas that are low in calories and high in protein to help keep blood sugar levels balanced. This book can be used by anyone to learn how to eat healthy even if they already are suffering from Type 2 diabetes.

The book has everything you need for your diabetic diet, including information about the food's type of carbohydrates and how healthy it is if you have type 2 diabetes. It also includes breakfast, lunch, and dinner ideas that are low in calories and high in protein to help keep blood sugar levels balanced. This book can be used by anyone to learn how to eat healthy even if they already are suffering from Type 2 diabetes.

The recipes in this cookbook will help you better understand the effect of food on your blood sugar levels and the way your body processes food. You can avoid foods that induce an increase in glucose and/or insulin levels, which can lead to Type 2 Diabetes, by keeping track of what you put into your body. The recipes in this book are designed to be simple, so everyone can enjoy them regardless of their cooking skills or experience. With this cookbook, you will find a wide variety of recipes for breakfasts, lunches, dinners and desserts that are quick and easy to prepare but loaded with flavor and nutrients. This book also includes nutritional facts for each recipe, as well as tips and hints about what ingredients to use in order to control your blood sugar levels more effectively. This book will be a great addition to your kitchen and you will use it over and over again.

The recipes in this cookbook are designed with ingredients that are available everywhere, so you can prepare great food in a snap. In addition, the nutritional information included with each recipe helps you make choices based on your blood glucose level, blood pressure, weight goals and more.

This is one of the best diabetic cookbooks I've ever read or used. The recipes are easy to make, tasty, low in calories and very reasonable in price. I've never been able to make pancakes or waffles before, which is a real problem when living on a diabetic budget. I can now prepare them whenever I want at a reasonable cost and without having to worry about the high carb content.

My acquaintance has had diabetes for the past four years. Her menu is super strict and healthy as she does everything she can to keep her blood sugar numbers down. She loves the recipes from this book and has already made several from it. She said that she was pleased with the results but added that she still needed some more help than the book provides in terms of covering snacks, sweets, etc., from her diet. She made up for that by substituting items within the recipes found in this book. I'm going to order this for her for Christmas. I think she'll be more than happy to receive it.

When you have diabetes and you have certain foods you shouldn't eat, it can get a little confusing as to what is okay to eat and what isn't. This cookbook has helped me a lot by telling me which food ingredients are okay to use and which ones aren't. It has helped me make healthier choices when it comes to planning my meals and snacks so that my blood sugar levels don't go out of control.

I have type 2 diabetes and am in the middle of trying to lower my diabetes level. I have been trying to control this with my diet, exercise and medication. This cookbook has helped me with many of my food choices. The recipes are healthy and more importantly, they are tasty! I love them!! They do not take long to prepare as well, which is a plus!

The recipes in this cookbook will allow you to make healthier choices for meals and snacks. They are easy to follow, simple, satisfying and heart-healthy too. You will enjoy them because they contain many different ingredients that are readily available at any local grocery store or supermarket or from your favorite online vendor. You will want to use these recipes on a regular basis because they are easy to make and they contain just the right number of calories, carbohydrates and fat. By choosing the recipes in this book, you'll be able to eat healthy meals without having to spend a lot of time in your kitchen.

It's crucial to follow your doctor's diet recommendations if you've been diagnosed with type 2 diabetes.

Printed in Great Britain
by Amazon

20369331R00059